The River Is Here

To
Andy &
Marguerite!
Keep
Seeking!
in the River
in love
Melinda
Fish

Other Books by Melinda Fish

When Addiction Comes to Church: Helping Yourself and Others Move into Recovery

Adult Children and the Almighty: Recovering from the Wounds of a Dysfunctional Home

Restoring the Wounded Woman: Recovering from Heartache and Discouragement

I'm So Tired of Acting Spiritual: Peeling Back the Mask

The River Is Here

Receiving and Sustaining the Blessing of Revival

Melinda Fish

Chosen Books

A Division of Baker Book House Co
Grand Rapids, Michigan 49516

Published by Chosen Books
A division of Baker Book House Company
P.O. Box 6287, Grand Rapids, MI 49516-6287

Second printing, December 1997

Printed in the United States of America

Library of Congress Cataloging-in-Publication Data

Fish, Melinda.
    The river is here : receiving and sustaining the blessing of revival /
Melinda Fish.
        p. cm.
    Includes bibliographical references.
    ISBN 0-8007-9245-9 (paper)
    1. Toronto blessing. 2. Fish, Melinda. 3. Revivals. 4. Pentecostalism.
    5. Church renewal. 6. Spiritual life—Christianity.   I. Title.
    BR1644.7.F57 1996
    269′.24—dc20   96-3436

Unless otherwise noted, Scripture quotations are from the New American Standard Bible, © The Lockman Foundation 1960, 1962, 1963, 1968, 1971, 1972, 1973, 1975, 1977.

Scripture quotations identified NKJV are from The New King James Version. Copyright © 1979, 1980, 1982, Thomas Nelson, Inc., Publishers.

Scripture quotations identified RSV are from the Revised Standard Version of the Bible, copyright 1946, 1952, 1971, and 1973 by the Division of Christian Education of the National Council of the Churches of Christ in the United States of America.

Scripture quotations identified KJV are from the King James Version of the Bible.

For current information about all releases from Baker Book House, visit our web site:
http://www.bakerbooks.com

This book is dedicated to the memory of
John Garlington,
whose prophetic ministry deeply affected my life.
He was taken from us on January 16, 1986.

Through faith, though he is dead, he still speaks.
Hebrews 11:4

I shall fill your mouths with laughter, and you shall laugh in the face of the enemy. . . . And they shall wonder, "What is it?" But I, the Lord thy God, shall arise in My people, and not only shall I turn your captivity, but I shall fill your mouths with laughter! Your young men shall drink new wine as from bowls and their mouths will be filled with laughter. Your women shall eat the corn and be filled with great joy.

From a prophetic word given through John Garlington
May 12, 1982
Evangelistic Center Church
Kansas City, Missouri

Contents

Foreword

I first met Melinda Fish through one or two of her letters. Her way with words impressed me, and the obvious depth of thought behind her questions and insights. On meeting her in person, I remember thinking she was not at all what I expected, but rather an experienced yet humble woman of God who knew what perseverance and faithfulness in the Kingdom of God was all about. I count it a privilege to be one of her new friends.

This insightful book, written in a superb descriptive style, probes the depths of the issues that have to do with renewal and the current move of God. I find her honoring to the Word of God, to prophetic ministry and to her own church, congregation, husband and people. She has investigated the issues, based on years of pastoral experience, yet keeps her own heart receptive and transparent. Little wonder the Father has met her in a powerful, life-changing and refreshing way!

The testimonies of her and her husband, Bill, both of them seasoned pastors, are not unlike my own. Desperately wanting more from God, while at the same time having found hope deferred so often, they were reluctant to believe yet again for a touch from God. How sweet it is when one discovers that this is not only a real and powerful move of God, but He is exceeding all of our expectations, both in quality and quantity!

This book answers probing questions: Why Toronto? Why are we so skeptical, so reluctant, so resistant to change? Her chapter on "Preparing for the Blessing" is wonderfully helpful, informing sincere believers what to expect and offering much help to those having difficulty receiving God's loving, healing touch deep in their emotions and souls. I particularly like the foundational emphasis on our personal need to be healed and forgiven of life's hurts and wounds, so that with the beam out of our own eye, we can see clearly to receive the Father's blessing and then give it away, removing the speck from our brother's eye.

If you are interested in more of God's love and empowerment, this book is a must-read, full of in-depth understanding, embellished with personal struggle and testimony of God's overcoming grace. I recommend it to you highly.

John Arnott, pastor
Toronto Airport Christian Fellowship

Expressions of Thanks

J wish to express my gratitude to the following friends who have helped this book come into being:

My husband, Bill.

My children, Sarah and Bill.

Stuart and Irene Bell, who arranged the meeting in Cobham with Britain's apostolic leaders, who gave hours of interviews, received us at their church and inspired me to greater unity in the Body of Christ.

Nick and Carol D'Amico, who gave me the use of their vacation home in the mountains.

Beverly Watt, who took responsibilities from me so I could have time to write.

Jack and Tricia Groblewski, New Covenant Christian Community, Bethlehem, Pennsylvania, for helping me with interviews and advice and who received me warmly as a friend.

Gerald Coates, David Holden, Peter Lyne and Roger Forster, apostolic team leaders in Great Britain, who set aside time to grant me interviews and encourage us in the Lord. Just watching them together made my heart ache for unity in the Body of Christ in America!

John and Carol Arnott, senior pastors of Toronto Airport Christian Fellowship, who walk in God's love and then give it away.

Steve Long, pastoral administrator at Toronto Airport Christian Fellowship, for the lengthy interview that taught me much about nurturing the blessing!

Ron Dick, whose simple act of faithfulness to the Lord in being there to pray for me in Toronto changed the course of my life and set in motion the chain of events that led to this book.

Dr. Guy Cheveau of the Toronto Airport Christian Fellowship for helping me understand the historical and biblical context for revival.

Church of the Risen Saviour, Trafford, Pennsylvania, who received the blessing of the Lord with open hearts.

Toronto Airport Christian Fellowship, for their tireless giving to the Body of Christ.

John Crane, pastor of Evangelistic Center Church, Kansas City, Missouri, for encouragement and prayers.

Kevin and Pam Swadling, directors of Christ for the Nations, U.K., for their love and friendship, and especially for going with us to Toronto the first time and letting us stay with them in England.

The gracious people at Sunderland Christian Centre, Sunderland, England, for their prayers, ministry and encouragement—especially Anthony Busk, for exhorting us with the Scriptures and praying for us.

Martin and Maureen Down and Stephen and Pippa Mawditt of St. George's Parish, Saham Toney, England, for encouragement and prayers.

Dick and Barbara Olson, who tried to tell me about the blessing five months before I experienced it, but I was too proud to listen!

Barbara Sambrooks, staff of Christ for the Nations, U.K., for her research on the issues relating to the "Toronto Blessing."

Pastor A. J. Rowden, for nurturing in me the vision for revival.

Steve and Cathy Dudgeon, Toronto Airport Christian Fellowship Bookstore, for their prayers and support.

Mary and Elliott Tepper, for their contributions and scriptural perspectives.

The following people who granted permission for interviews and testimonies: Drs. Marie and Lowell Hoffman, Peter Jackson, John Carr, Roberta Crane, David Edwards, Rick Leis, George and Joanne Stockhowe, Earl and Veral Roundtree, Jennie and Paul Blackham, Jim Arth, Shirley and Ron Nardina, Melissa Antolec, Linda Pacifico, Debra Petrosky, Gary and Donna Paladin, Nancy Westerberg, Bill Westerberg, Ruth Madeira, Tiffany Sines, Tim Decker, Edye, Joseph Garlington, Gary Mitrick, Dr. Sheila Johnson-Hunt, and others who want to remain anonymous!

Jane Campbell, who edited this book and gave me wise counsel about the presentation of these facts.

1

The River

On November 24, 1994, about 6:30 P.M., Ron Dick started the engine of his '91 Mercury Sable and began the 35-minute drive to his church, the Toronto Airport Vineyard, that he had made three nights a week for months. As the freeway from his home in Oakville, Ontario, stretched out before him, he did not know that his faithfulness to his post on the prayer team was about to put him on a collision course with a hungry pastor and family who were especially desperate for a touch from God.

For nearly twenty years, that pastor and his wife had been waiting for revival that had been promised them by nearly every guest speaker who had stood in the pulpit of their church in western Pennsylvania. By this time the hills and valleys of hope and subsequent disappointment had left them so skeptical that they little expected the power of God to move in their lives in any meaningful way.

From the States, where it was Thanksgiving evening, several hundred American citizens had crossed the Canadian border to spend the holiday in Toronto. The service was not unlike the hundreds of services that had taken place six nights a week since January 20, 1994, when the Holy Spirit had fallen on a sparse crowd. On that January night, Randy Clark, a Vineyard pastor from St. Louis, had been invited by John and Carol Arnott, pastors of the Airport Vineyard, to begin a series of meetings in the church that met in a strip of businesses on Dixie Drive in Mississauga, Ontario, a few hundred yards from the airport runway. Randy, unsure he had enough messages to complete the short series of meetings, had brought two staff members with him, hoping they could fill in when he ran out of sermons.

But Randy did not run out of sermons. The power of the Holy Spirit fell that night in an unusual way. One by one members of the church began to laugh, cry, shake and fall to the carpet under the influence of the Holy Spirit. This happened the next night, too, and the next.

News of the unusual phenomena spread quickly throughout churches in surrounding Ontario. Within days pastors were attending to see if God was truly there. News also spread through the secular press in Britain. Soon both curious and spiritually dry believers from all over the world were booking flights to Toronto. Two airlines, AirCanada and British Airways, had to add extra flights from London to accommodate the widening flow of seekers.

Word of the outbreak of something unusual reached the ears of those in the United States who read about it in a handful of periodicals, secular and Christian (including *Charisma*). Many believers heard about the unusual phenomena through negative reports from a nationally syndicated radio broadcast. So many seekers made their way to the Airport Vineyard in 1994 that *Toronto Life* magazine named the church Toronto's number-one tourist venue for that year.

On this November night, as an eager congregation crowded into the lobby of the Asian Trade Center in Toronto (later to become the permanent home of the burgeoning fellowship), a young pastor, the son of a Baptist minister, began his message with a prayer: "Come, Holy Spirit!" Then he opened his Bible to Numbers 11 and began to speak about Moses, the seventy elders, and Eldad and Medad who prophesied in the camp as the Holy Spirit fell on the leaders Moses had selected to help him.

In many ways Ron Dick, the driver of the Mercury Sable and a member of the prayer team, was like Eldad or Medad—an ordinary guy. Retiring early after an accident crushed his back, Ron wanted his later years to count for Jesus Christ. Years before he had asked the Lord to allow him to be "in on the next move of God." Earlier in

1994, Ron and his wife, Nancy, had heard about the moving of the Holy Spirit at the Toronto Airport Vineyard and joined one of the church's home groups. Soon he volunteered for the prayer team, hoping the Lord would use him to spread the blessing to others.

After a period of worship, as the evening message began, one side of the congregation in the 2,500-seat auditorium began to erupt in a wave of laughter. After the message ended, people were asked to stack their chairs and line up in rows for prayer. They did; hundreds stood waiting patiently for something.

Then prayer team members began to make their way through the crowd. Ron Dick sought those who looked ready to receive prayer and began to lay hands gently on each one. The power of God began to overcome one after another in the crowd, as it had for months. Soon the majority of the nearly two thousand people present were lying on the floor. Some were laughing while others were crying out, shaking or weeping. Others lay quietly as though engaged in prayer. A few stood transfixed like oak trees by a river, soaking quietly in the Lord's presence.

After a few minutes Ron stopped in front of a middle-aged couple—the pastor and his wife from Pennsylvania. He touched the wife on her forehead so lightly that she could hardly feel it. But a few seconds later she, too, was lying on the carpet, swept off her feet for the first time in her life by the power of the Holy Spirit.

When she and her husband returned to the States two days later, the renewal they had expected for more than two decades finally broke out in their church.

I will always be grateful to Ron Dick and all the people at that church (now called the Toronto Airport Christian Fellowship) because my husband, Bill, and I were the couple.

Where We Came From

It had taken the Lord several months to break through our skepticism. Like other pastors, we had grown weary of expecting and not seeing. The Body of Christ in the United States has gone through a particularly dark period that began in the late 1980s. In spite of a continuous trickle of salvations, the charismatic movement that made the '70s a glorious decade in modern Church history had waned, and the receding wave had exposed the debris—scandals created by the impure motives of those who tried to capitalize on God's power. Church attendance fell off nationally. Boredom put churchgoers to sleep as frustrated pastors resorted to seminars and programs to motivate believers to faithfulness.

Bill and I were no exception. In 1976 we moved from Dallas to Pittsburgh to take the pastorate of a small, inner-city congregation. Before we left Texas, Bill had an actual vision. He saw a mighty river of water forming as the snow on a mountaintop melted. The force of the water built up behind a dam on the mountainside, forming a crack. At first a large teardrop of water oozed through the crack, but soon the force of the water burst the dam, and the mighty river flowed down the mountainside. In the next scene, Bill saw the river begin to trickle out the front doors of a small, weather-beaten church building in the middle of a desert. As the water began to flow, the river became deeper and wider until it covered the desert. Finally, on the banks of the river, signs of life began to appear.

After our arrival in Pittsburgh, a pastor we knew from Dallas came to visit and felt God impressing him with a Scripture passage for us that included these verses:

> "Do not call to mind the former things, or ponder things of the past. Behold, I will do something new, now it will spring forth; will you not be aware of it? I will even make a roadway in the wilderness, rivers in the desert. . . . I have given waters in the wilderness and rivers in the desert, to give drink to My chosen people."
>
> Isaiah 43:18–20

A few months later, in a bookstore that was closing, Bill found a copy of Arthur Wallis' classic on revival, *In the Day of Thy Power.* As he flipped through it, one passage caught his attention. On page 47 was a description of the same vision Bill had seen before leaving Dallas.

"In picture language," Wallis wrote, "this is revival."

But he went on, "Often in the period just preceding the movement, the stream of power and blessing has been unusually low. The people of God and the work of God have been in great affliction and reproach, despised or ignored by those around them."

This is the desert.

In one of my previous books, *Restoring the Wounded Woman* (Chosen, 1993), I described the emotional upheaval Christians often face when their heartfelt desires and prayers go unanswered. In the wake of repeated disappointment and deferred hope, the heartsick Christian often lapses into depression and despair. The result is what I call the barrenness syndrome.

The barrenness syndrome is characterized by an inability to bear natural or spiritual fruit. It is also characterized by shame, since prayers and faithfulness seem to remain unrewarded. Christians with the barrenness syndrome, weighed down by a constant sense of shame before others, may also feel victimized by God through the common reverses of life. They may become angry with Him and withdraw from fellowship, since they have had their hopes revived and crushed repeatedly and are afraid to stir up hope even one more time.

Causes of the barrenness syndrome are as numerous as the individuals who suffer with it. Each personal dream that goes unfulfilled, each hope or prayer shattered by situations beyond the believer's control, may lie at the root. Fruitlessness is one of the most severe tests of a Christian's life—one that all of us face in some area.

For many believers, the past several years have brought a sense of barrenness. Between 1976 and 1994 Bill and I became all too familiar with it. We held out hope and faced disappointment when every year for twenty years failed to bring the hoped-for revival. Although the church in Pittsburgh had been established, it remained small. And although we arrived with hope and faith, after nearly two decades we faced the possibility that revival might not come to pass, that we had been somehow mistaken or that we had been driven only by naïve enthusiasm.

The pastoral staff met often to discuss what we would do if we could not find enough volunteers to staff the Sunday school classes. We usually lacked enough money to pay the salaries. We were accustomed to smallness and the fact that the baptistry had not been filled with water in years. Growth was limited to dissatisfied believers migrating to our church from other congregations. We derived our sense of self-worth as a congregation from mission trips devoted to helps ministries for missionaries on the field. But when we considered the lack, we were overwhelmed by our sense of powerlessness and the shortage of resources to accomplish the task.

Bill and I seemed caught in a cycle of discouragement with the congregation. When we were up, they were down, and when they were up, we were down. In 1993 we spent long periods in soul-searching. It was the lowest point in my Christian life. I endured major surgery, hormone shock and began to experience panic attacks. The future, I feared, would resemble the past—and that thought brought waves of depression and fear.

Bill and I determined that we could wait no longer. We had let our dream die of seeing God's blessing on our church, and now we sent résumés out of state in the hopes that the Lord would take this as His cue to open another door. We had lost our vision.

People in this condition cannot pray with expectancy for revival. Something must happen to revive their spirits so that they can believe. Hunger for God must be reignited by the Lord Himself.

But when we arrived in Toronto, accompanied by our fifteen-year-old son, Bill, we realized to our amazement that we were not alone in our despair. Thousands of pastors from Tasmania to Finland, from Korea to South Africa, had also lost their vision or faced trials equally devastating. They were crawling to Ontario in the hopes that God would revive them.

But does any Scripture passage indicate that an omnipresent God confines Himself to manifesting His presence in one location more than another?

Why Toronto?

In 1 Samuel 19 King Saul, angry and jealous of David, not only threatened David's life but tried on two occasions to murder him. David fled in fear to the prophet Samuel in Ramah. But Saul, intent on killing David, sent messengers to where Samuel and his school of prophets were meeting and prophesying. As the messengers entered the area, they, too, began to prophesy, rendering them incapable of carrying out Saul's orders. This happened to three sets of messengers. Finally Saul decided to get David himself. But as he entered the area, he fell to the ground, stripped off his clothes and began to prophesy "all that day and all that night" (verse 24).

The powerful presence of God had been manifested at a certain location for a certain purpose.

The church in Toronto has seen seeker and skeptic alike fall under the influence of the Holy Spirit's presence and experience unusual manifestations. Every time God brings revival, there is usually a visible outpouring, as happened ninety years ago during the Azusa Street revival in Los Angeles. The Holy Spirit fell on a church across the tracks meeting in a mission at 312 Azuse Street. For blocks around the Lord seemed to have set aside a radius devoted to His presence. Unbelievers who entered that area were drawn inexplicably to the meeting and converted.

But I am asked whether it is necessary to go to Toronto. "Can't God move on me where I am?" I reply that if they faced the possibility of dying in the middle of a desert and realized that an oasis was not far away, to what lengths would they go in order to find it?

Why visitation comes in one place and not another is known only to God. Still, it is only natural to wonder why He moves in one place first. Did people there do something to warrant the blessing?

Supernatural revival falls on people, I believe, not because they earn it, but because they need it. When John Arnott, pastor of the Toronto Airport Christian Fellowship, is asked why the Lord chose his church in Ontario on which to pour out His renewal, he sometimes replies, "Because it's near the airport." Then he confesses freely he does not know why. The staff and members did not expect to host a "ground-zero" visitation beginning in 1994, nor do they feel they did something to merit the favor of God. Like Mary, the mother of Jesus, they were surprised. They were not hungrier for God or praying more than anyone else. They simply wanted the Lord and had promised Him not to quench the Holy Spirit if and when He came.

In the days before matches, John Arnott points out, there were two ways to start a fire. You could stand there and rub two sticks together, or you could go to your neighbor who already had a fire burning and take a coal back to your fireplace. Bill and I were too weary to rub sticks. When we heard that fire had fallen in Toronto, we decided to go. Cold, tired and hungry, we set out to investigate the things we had been told.

This book, then, is about the river of blessing that has sprung up in our day—a river that has begun to flow in many places throughout the world. Although the fountainhead seems to have been a church in Toronto, this river is actually flowing from the presence of the heavenly Father. At the end of the day, it will not matter where it started. What matters is that you realize God wants to direct His river through you to the dry places around you. When God's river flows, it is no longer necessary to pray for it, but rather to recognize it and open your life and the doors of your church to the blessing of the Holy Spirit.

But recognizing a real move of the Spirit is not always easy, especially in the beginning. In fact, the river of God's visitation often resembles the way Jesus Christ came the first time. A visitation often has a small beginning in an obscure place like Bethlehem.

This book is about what happens when the Lord visits His Church. The word *visitation* in Greek is derived from the verb *episkeptomai*, which means "to inspect, to go to see." In every season of visitation, the Lord goes to see His Church, to look her over. Is she ready for His coming, to be His dwelling place?

Examine with me the current renewal sweeping the Church. In it are keys to understanding how God moves in days of true visitation. What are the earmarks of genuine revival, so that we may not be like the Pharisees of Jesus' day and miss the day of visitation? Is there a scriptural basis for the unusual demonstrations of power? We will explore how a visitation challenges the wineskin of every local church and tests her ability to conform to the new thing God is doing. We will see how great leaders in Church history experienced their own days of visitation and how leaders are responding to the current renewal. Where will it take you and your local church?

Above all, how can you open your heart to recognize your own day of visitation?

2

Is It the Real Thing?

One Sunday morning not long before our trip to the Toronto Airport Vineyard, something unusual happened in our church. Linda Bock, the nineteen-year-old daughter of one of our deacons, was singing with the worship team as usual on a Sunday morning. As the congregation paused between songs, Linda began to laugh and cry at the same time. In the back of the auditorium, her father stood up and (since we are a charismatic church that believes in the gifts of the Holy Spirit for today) gave a message in tongues.

To my surprise, the interpretation flashed through my own mind immediately like words on a tickertape. It impressed me that the Lord was saying this:

I want to come into the church and do things you have never seen Me do before, use people you have never seen Me use before, and touch people in ways I have never done before. All I want to know is, do I have your permission?

We all clapped and said, "Yes, Lord!"

But about a month later, when Bill and I got back from Toronto, God actually showed up. He was hard to recognize at first, and how He came was unlike anything I expected.

The Effect

The Wednesday evening after Bill and I returned from the Airport Vineyard, we called all the members of the church together to discuss what was going on in Toronto. Several had already been influenced by the syndicated radio program that was issuing negative, even erroneous reports about the meetings there. They felt skeptical, to say the least. But as we shared what we had seen, a special sense of God's presence began to hover over our small congregation.

Our son, Bill, testified about his experience in Toronto. He, too, had been on the floor under the power of the Holy Spirit. He amazed everyone by associating this experience with things God had promised our congregation in years past.

"God told us that it's springtime in the Church," Bill said fervently, "and this is it. You sow seeds in the spring. God is sowing seeds for the harvest with what is happening now."

Until that moment we had no idea our teenage son had been meditating on the prophetic words spoken to our congregation.

One by one other members of the church began to worship, pray and weep under the sovereign power of the Holy Spirit. It was as though the Lord was once again indicating His intent to come in and do "something new."

The following Wednesday night, my husband called everyone forward who wanted to receive prayer. Bill had experienced no external manifestation himself while we were in Toronto, other than quiet weeping. Now, as he prayed for the members of our congregation, he purposely did not touch them for fear of being accused of pushing them over. Yet as he prayed for them, one after the other began to drop to the floor as if overcome gently by the Lord's unseen hand.

We were amazed not only that they were falling, but at the ones who were falling—those we least expected to succumb to "emotional displays."

The first person to go down was Nancy Westerberg, for ten years our faithful children's pastor. She has a quiet, reserved demeanor but had been in a depression for several months. Now her petite frame hit the floor at the same time that her feet began to move up and down as though she were drum-rolling them on the carpet. Her arms began to sway back and forth in the air. This went on for several minutes. Suddenly she jumped up and took my hands. "Dance with me, Melinda!"

I was startled but did not know what else to do. Nancy and I twirled around the sanctuary.

Nancy's depression, she told us later, lifted immediately. For nights afterward, even in her sleep, she would feel her feet beginning to dance. Her heart had begun to dance, too. This was December 1994. The depression has not returned.

Suddenly we understood why the Lord had asked our permission to move in His own way. He was, He said, going to touch people as He had not done before. The blessing would come with some humbling manifestations. We had a choice to make: Were we willing to pay the price of being thought of as strange, or would we stop these emotional outbreaks and risk quenching the Holy Spirit?

The River

For years Bill and I had held onto the Scripture passage that our minister friend from Dallas had given us at the outset of our ministry in Pittsburgh: "I will do something new, now it will spring forth. . . . I will even make a roadway in the wilderness, rivers in the desert . . ." (Isaiah 43:19). But I never considered the fact that throughout Scripture, rivers are places of testing.

The Jordan was a testing place for Naaman the Syrian before it was a place of blessing (see 2 Kings 5). Infected with leprosy, the commander of the Syrian army had heard that a prophet in Israel could heal. But Israel was Syria's enemy. Comparable to Naaman's dilemma would be Saddam Hussein having to come to Pittsburgh for a liver transplant. When Elisha sent Naaman to the Jordan to dip seven times, the commander was angry. Happily for him, his servants persuaded him to humble himself. He was healed on the seventh dip.

Earlier, when Gideon's army was being chosen for battle against the Midianites, the Lord told him to take the men to the river (see Judges 7). The means they used to drink the water determined whether or not they were selected for battle.

It is no coincidence that the metaphor for the current visitation of God is the river. Although the waters of a river are refreshing and life-giving, they bring fear to the hearts of many. As their course deepens and becomes more forceful, those who are afraid of rising water head for dry ground.

Every revival in church history has been accompanied by unusual manifestations. There is no such thing as a revival without "mess." The messy aspects of revival are usually the characteristics that draw attention to it and signal a change in the seasons of God. The mess is an affront to tradition, which has been established in part by what happened during the last move of God. If weeping and repentance were the earmarks of the previous revival, then those acquainted with that movement tend to expect tearful repentance in the next move of God. But what if God changes gears? What if the familiar earmarks are not prominent? This has the unsettling effect of making the revival unrecognizable to those who are unable to change.

To have been an active part of one move of God, therefore, does not ensure that you will be part of the next. Church history is full of examples. Followers of Luther drowned the Anabaptists; Anglicans persecuted Methodists; mainline denominations opposed the Assemblies of God; the Pentecostals opposed the Latter Rain movement. Be sure that many who were involved in the charismatic renewal will oppose what comes next.

But these are days to be humble rather than critical. When the flood of God comes, it destroys manmade objects in its way—but we may not know which objects are manmade until the river hits them. Jesus cautioned all of us to build our houses on the rock, because wind, rain and floods may break out against them and cause them to fall. Interestingly, each of these metaphors—wind, rain and floods—is commonly used to describe revival. All these natural phenomena, as well as a river raging out of its banks, are beyond the control of human beings.

Something New

For years I quoted the phrase *something new* with regard to the revival I prayed for, while I assumed subconsciously that what would happen would repeat what happened in previous revivals.

My own idea was birthed in Baptist tradition. To us revival was not real unless people engaged in open confession of sin, repentance with tears, and public salvation or rededication of their lives to the Lord. Revival usually occurred in scheduled meetings that lasted for a few days. Often we would go to the altar, weep, feel the effects for a while, then return to business as usual at church. No alterations were ever made in our church program, other than yearly changes in calendar events and volunteer personnel. It never occurred to us that we should expect God to move in any other way.

Then, in the early 1970s, while Bill was in seminary, we saw a visitation of the Lord that brought spiritual renewal to Beverly Hills Baptist Church in Dallas. People could sense the presence of the Lord even in the empty auditorium. Before services the crowd overflowed out the doors and into the lobby. More than once, unbelievers who did not intend to go to church were drawn in off the sidewalk as they passed by the building. Sometimes people were at the altar even before the choir came in at the beginning of the service, under conviction of sin and committing their lives to Christ.

To witness the impact of that visitation was powerful. I still remember almost 25 years later the awesome sense of God's presence that enveloped us all and equipped us for service. Supplementing the memory of revival meetings from my childhood, now I framed *this* experience in my mind as true revival: weeping, repentance, people being touched by the Holy Spirit, the irresistible grace of God, perhaps a few miraculous healings to kick everything off and attract the lost. If a visitation by God was real revival, I assumed, the church would fill quickly with new believers.

Letting go of this as the only model for real revival is difficult. I imagined myself during the coming revival (whenever it came) as ready to be used to lead others into a relationship with Jesus. After all, I had known Him for decades, had been filled with the Holy Spirit more than twenty years before, and had endured the dry season faithfully. Besides, I had read many books about revival and was certain that when it broke out, I would recognize and embrace it quickly.

But I was not prepared at all for what happened. In fact, initially I rejected it because it was not what I expected.

The first thing I had heard was that "holy laughter" had broken out in a church that our friends Dick and Barbara Olsen attended in Wilmington, North Carolina, and in another one in Chichester, England. Jane Campbell, my editor, told me about laughter breaking out in other areas of the Body of Christ. These friends broached the subject cautiously, knowing Bill and I did not go in for fads.

Why, I wondered, would God do something like that? Laughter was naturally contagious, too easy to mimic. Besides, laughter seemed out of place in a world with so much sorrow, a world that needed the Gospel so desperately.

Nor did Bill and I place any value on falling in response to prayer. We had seen many people fall from the power of suggestion or be given a shove by an overeager evangelist. Too many, in our opinion, were like the Roman guards who came to the Garden of Gethsemane to take Jesus away. They fell under the power of Jesus' presence, but got up and arrested Him anyway. Falling did not seem to have a prominent place in Scripture, and we did not see enough fruit from it to seek such an experience ourselves.

These were the reasons we always gave for resisting "emotional experiences"—in this case, holy laughter and falling under the power of the Spirit. But deeply embedded in our minds was a rigidly defined framework for what revival and church life should be like. This framework was created more by our previous experience than by Scripture. And it suggests how tradition is formed: by doing things the way we always have, without considering change.

Tradition is also formed by what never happens. Because we may never have seen something—a miracle, for example—we cannot believe it, so we feel compelled to develop a theology based on why there are no such things as miracles. Or we get used to "doing church" in the context of our particular denomination and assume that, at least for us, it will always be that way. If God wants to get to us, He must work within the box we have drawn for Him.

But when revival comes, God does not necessarily accommodate our traditions that interfere with His purposes for the moment. He begins to take His divine crayons and color outside the lines. When God says He will do something new, why do we assume it will be something we have seen before? We seem to think He will surprise only unbelievers. Unfortunately many sincere believers, even those who have been seeking the Lord for revival for years, often miss the day.

Why Do We Miss the Day of Visitation?

Jesus wept over Jerusalem, the promised city full of religious people:

> "If you had known in this day, even you, the things which make for peace! But now they have been hidden from your eyes. . . . They will not leave in you one stone upon another, because you did not recognize the time of your visitation."
>
> Luke 19:42, 44

Is it possible to be in God's presence and not know it? Won't I be able to recognize the real power of the Holy Spirit? But the Pharisees of Jesus' day could not or would not, even though they knew the Scriptures thoroughly.

There are several reasons we can miss a move of God.

Resistance to Change

Soon after renewal broke out in our church, I attended a motivational seminar sponsored by the realtors from several local offices in our franchise. The speaker showed a video on the subject of human reaction to change, which pointed out that the initial natural response of human beings to any form of change is usually negative. The video offered as examples several scientific breakthroughs made by obscure people working every day at their jobs. Because these people were "common" workers and not perceived as innovators, their inventions and discoveries were rejected at first at the executive levels of their companies. In fact, the workers, rather than being praised and promoted, were actually shown the door.

One example of resistance to change took place when the seat of the watchmaking industry was still Switzerland. A workman in a Swiss factory discovered that a quartz crystal, cut in a certain way, could be vibrated at a certain frequency and made to run a watch. But the executives of his company, unable to see value in such a discovery, discarded it. Whoever heard of a watch you do not have to wind? It took the Japanese to buy the idea of a quartz watch and revolutionize the watchmaking industry.

Tradition has the power to hold back blessing when it blocks our vision and prevents us from making the necessary paradigm shift so we can appreciate and implement change. In the same way, revival tests the theology and flexibility of the Church to recognize and yield to the power of the Holy Spirit.

Preconceived Ideas of Revival

I have already shared that I nearly missed this current blessing because what was happening did not fit my idea of what a revival should be like.

A few months after renewal commenced in our congregation, I traveled to Arizona to speak in a church there. After the meetings, I was with some pastors in a restaurant when they ran into another pastor who had returned recently from Toronto.

This clergyman, who had been involved in the Latter Rain movement in the 1950s (a revival characterized by healings and miracles), had attended two or three evening services at the Toronto Airport Christian Fellowship. He offered the following assessment to us in the restaurant: "They don't know what they're doing up there. It's nothing we haven't seen before. And anyhow, they won't be able to hold onto it. I handled it by writing a report and handing it out to my congregation."

His attitude reminded me of the ten spies who came out of Canaan with a negative report. All I could think in response to his assessment was, *For God so loved the world, that He did not send a report.*

I could not resist sharing with this pastor my own reactions to the current move of God. My testimony, I hoped, would inspire him to take a second look.

"Our experience was completely different," I told him and the other ministers at the table. "For my husband and me, the power of the Holy Spirit has been life-giving and refreshing and brought the beginning of a long-awaited season of blessing. When we returned to our church, we decided to open the doors to it. And the Lord has actually revived our congregation through it."

But he did not seem open or even interested. I realized then that, except for the Lord's mercy to me, I would have had the same attitude.

In order to recognize the Lord's presence when He comes to visit, we must be willing to give up preconceived notions about revival that are shaped by experiences of the past. Remember that passage from Isaiah: "Do not call to mind the former things, or ponder things of the past" (Isaiah 43:18).

The pastor in the restaurant could not open his heart because his idea of revival was limited to the way God moved in the Latter Rain. To him, revival meant healing, prophesying, salvation and baptism in the Holy Spirit. He wanted to hear the old songs and see God act in precisely the same manner to the younger generation.

Christians from a non-charismatic or non-Pentecostal background look for revival differently. But the assessment of any of these may be similar to that of the people of Jesus' day: "Can anything good come out of Toronto?"

Toronto is not the only place renewal is occurring, of course. The blessing of God has been moving, starting in one church in southern Ontario, all over the world.

Sometimes we flee to the Scriptures for refuge from the rising water. The Pharisees tried this, too. But with their hardened hearts, they overlooked certain prophetic passages. They did not expect a Savior to come from a poor family. They expected a warrior who would judge like the Gideons and Joshuas of the past. So through what glasses are we reading Scripture? I have been amazed to sift practically every experience common to this renewal through Scripture and find evidence in its pages. (We will look at this evidence in chapter 4.)

In Christian tradition, certain myths arise like proverbs and govern our analysis of whether or not a movement is from God. We cite certain criteria as though they are Scripture. We say, for example, "The Holy Spirit never interrupts Himself." In fact, the Holy Spirit interrupted Peter's message to Cornelius' friends with a demonstration of power: "While Peter was still speaking these words. . ." (Acts 10:44).

Another "proverb" we quote is, "If something is from God, you won't be afraid." But every time an angel appeared to anyone in Scripture, the person was terrified and the angel had to reassure him.

We also say, "If it's God, you'll be able to understand it." But when Jesus ascended into heaven, He left the disciples scratching their heads about many things He had said. He had even told them, "I have many more things to say to you, but you cannot bear them now. But when He, the Spirit of truth, comes. . ." (John 16:12–13).

I have read numerous articles decrying the fact that what is happening now is not really a revival. Real revival is supposed to look another way, and we should not play this up bigger than it is. It is as if they are saying, "This may be God, but I don't believe I need it. I'll wait for something more powerful, something closer to my definition, to come along."

Who are we to diminish anything God is doing? Can't God do something new in His Church? Perhaps He is accomplishing His ends with unusual means. Perhaps He is again doing something as non-traditional as His healing of the man born blind (see John 9). He spit on dirt and anointed the man's eyes with "mud" to enable him to see, offending Jewish tradition on the Sabbath. The end was worth the means to everyone but the Pharisees.

Honest Skepticism

Another reason we may miss a move of God is honest skepticism. Luke praised the Bereans for being "more noble-minded than those in Thessalonica" (Acts 17:11) because they examined the Scriptures daily in response to Paul's message, to see if these things were so. Healthy skepticism is born of a sincere heart that truly wants God and is willing to search out the truth and acknowledge if God is there. No one wants to fall into error through gullibility.

How is it possible, then, to discern whether a move is of God before you commit to it? Sometimes you will not know until you jump into the river and experience it yourself.

Dr. Howard Ervin, then a pastor from New Jersey, had similar advice for John Sherrill, at that time a non-Christian reporter analyzing the spiritual phenomenon of tongues:

> "Let me tell you a little story. I happen to be fond of church architecture. One day when I was out driving, I found an exquisite little Gothic chapel. I stopped my car and got out to admire it. But that little church happened to have at its entrance a bright red door. My eyes would try to follow the soaring lines of the building upward as Gothic architecture makes you do, but every time they were jerked back to that red door. It was so flamboyant, it kept me from seeing the whole picture.
>
> "Tongues, John, are like that door. As long as you stand outside, your attention is going to be riveted there and you're not going to be able to see anything else. Once you go through, however, you are surrounded by the thousand wonders of light and sound and form that the architect intended. You look around and that door isn't even red on the inside. It's there. It's to be used. But it has taken its proper place in the design of the whole church.
>
> "That's what I'd hope for you, John. I think it's time for you to walk through that door. If you really want to discover what the Pentecostal experience is all about, don't concentrate on tongues, but step through the door and meet the Holy Spirit."
>
> *They Speak with Other Tongues*
> (Chosen, 1985), pp. 114–115

To step through the door, to jump into the river, takes courage. And being willing to acknowledge later that we have been mistaken is humbling indeed.

Bill and I went to Toronto because an Episcopal priest and his wife that we know, George and Joanne Stockhowe, encouraged us to do it. They had attended services there for a week and written a favorable newsletter to thirty of their friends. They took time to point out certain Scripture texts and mention things that were said from the pulpit of the Airport Fellowship. One point that caught my attention: Joanne's observation that there were no "stars" at that church, no glittering personalities, only nameless people who were refreshed by what God seemed to be doing there.

So we decided to investigate. Like the shepherds who were told of Jesus' birth on the hillside near Bethlehem, we said to ourselves, "Let us go to Bethlehem [or, in this case, Toronto] and see this thing which has come to pass." I fully believed that if it was really a visitation of the Lord, He would let me know.

By the time we arrived, I sensed that unless I was touched by the Lord soon in a refreshing way, I would never be able to fulfill His plan for my life. I was, I realized, "wretched and miserable and poor and blind and naked" (Revelation 3:17).

At the Wednesday morning ministers' session, Dr. Guy Chevreau, a Baptist minister from Ontario, was speaking about the historical significance of the unusual manifestations that had accompanied this outbreak of the Holy Spirit's power. Like any pastor, I needed to hear that these manifestations were biblical and had happened to others in Church history. I was relieved to learn that throughout Church history there had been numerous manifestations of jerking, laughing, fainting, crying out and other noisy activities in response to outbreaks of God's power. I was surprised to learn that John Wesley, the founder of Methodism, and his brother Charles, the great hymnwriter, were both overcome by holy laughter for more than an hour while walking through a field one day. The experience caused them to be full of the joy of the Lord's presence.

During the Great Awakening, similar manifestations occurred to the believers in the area of Northampton, Massachusetts, in 1735. Jonathan Edwards wrote in an essay entitled "A Narrative of Surprising Conversions" (quoted in *Edwards on Revival,* Banner of Truth Trust, 1994):

> It was very wonderful to see how persons' affections were sometimes moved—when God did as it were suddenly open their eyes, and let into their minds a sense of the greatness of His grace, the fullness of Christ, and his readiness to save—after having been broken with apprehensions of divine wrath, and sunk into an abyss under a sense of guilt which they were ready to think was beyond the mercy of God. Their joyful surprise has caused their hearts as it were to leap, so that they have been ready to break forth into laughter, tears often at the same time issuing like a flood, and intermingling a loud weeping.
>
> p. 37

As Guy Chevreau finished his talk, I knew that what was going on in this church could not possibly be all wrong, as some had reported. Nor could it be all the flesh, as others had surmised.

Throughout that first trip there, I scrutinized everything to make sure it was Christ-centered. If it was a true work of the Holy Spirit, I knew it would draw attention to Jesus Christ. Some eager reporters had so focused on the unusual manifestations that I had not been able to see how Jesus Christ was being honored. But as Bill and I listened to testimonies from the platform of those who had been touched in the renewal, we noticed one common thread: Christians who had been apathetic churchgoers like us had been transformed into lovers of Jesus Christ through the means of receiving prayer at every service from other believers. Those praying for others were people like Ron Dick (whom I mentioned in chapter 1)—not big-name speakers, but ordinary people who had themselves been touched by the Lord.

One woman's testimony called to my heart. She and her husband, chronic TV-watchers, had all but quit going to church. When one of her friends phoned to tell her God was moving at the Airport Vineyard, they went out of curiosity and received prayer. She wept as she testified how precious Jesus has become to her. While she talked, she "jerked" every few seconds. But I did not notice that as much as

I noticed how much she loved Jesus now, whereas before she had had no emotion for Him. It may have been her testimony, in fact, that made me want to receive prayer again.

Because I was not only curious; I was hungry. And when you are hungry, you can hardly resist going to see for yourself.

Jealousy, Pride, Fear

Sometimes our reluctance to go where God is reportedly pouring out His blessing is based not on spiritual skepticism, not on preconceived notions of what that blessing should be like, not even on financial lack, but on deep-seated jealousy or pride. Like Naaman the Syrian, we want another river back home to dip into, rather than the Jordan.

Another reason for opposition or resistance: fear. As the river deepens and becomes more forceful (as I pointed out earlier), those afraid of rising water head for dry ground.

Who Is in Control?

Not long after revival began to visit our church in Pennsylvania, a picture came to my mind as I meditated about God's will for us. I pictured Jesus standing at a doorway knocking on the door. But instead of wearing a flowing robe, He wore plumber's work clothes. Around His neck hung cables and chains. In each hand He held a toolbox. On His feet He wore muddy work boots. He was coming to fix things in people's lives in our church.

In this picture, I had just had neutral-colored carpet installed on the floor of a room I thought was part of my house. But here was Jesus with muddy boots wanting to come through the door! I wanted badly for Him to come in, but not like that! Where was the beautiful Jesus with light, glory and cleanliness? I had the impulse to put down plastic in front of Him.

Then I realized it was as though I were telling the Lord of glory where He could and could not step in His own house. He was coming to help

me, but with "no beauty that we should desire him" (Isaiah 53:2, KJV).
I realized I could make the same mistake the Pharisees did: not recognizing Jesus because He was not as I thought He should be.

No, I said, *I would much rather have the muddy footprints of Jesus than no footprints at all.*

Are you ready for Jesus to come in and repair your heart? Opening the door to Jesus in this renewal may cost you. Some people will not understand it and will never accept it. Revival comes on God's terms, not ours. "God in revival does not take sides," said John Wesley (quoted in Robert Tuttle's *John Wesley: His Life and Theology,* Zondervan/Asbury, 1978). "He takes over." Isn't it time the Lord's leaders let Him have control of His Church again?

Jumping into the river of God means letting go of control. It involves risk. But then, everything worth having—including the visitation presence of the Lord—involves risk. All we need to know is that it is God. After that, there should be no question as to whether we surrender.

Let's take a closer look at the river itself. What kind of blessing is it bringing?

3

What Does It Mean?

*A*s the Lord began to move in our congregation, giving us a new sense of His presence and power, we faced the same questions that confronted the onlookers on the Day of Pentecost. In their amazement and perplexity, they cried out, "Whatever could this mean?" (Acts 2:12, NKJV). It is the response of the Israelites to the manna God sent from heaven to feed them in the wilderness. In fact, the very word *manna* means "What is it?"

Asking what something means is a natural reaction as our human understanding searches for a way to process the workings of a God who has suddenly broken out of our control and invaded our "normal" lives with something unexplainable.

Since the renewal with its accompanying signs has spread to churches all over the world, we can recognize certain earmarks of what has become known as the "Toronto Blessing." But first let's look at the blessing itself.

What Is the Blessing?

The "blessing" is a refreshing wave of the Holy Spirit that is empowering congregations with a renewed sense of the heavenly Father's love and power. It was named the "Toronto Blessing" by the British press who saw the outpouring on the congregation at Holy Trinity,

Brompton (HTB), an Anglican church in London's Knightsbridge section, across the street from the famous Harrods department store.

In May 1994 Ellie Mumford, wife of John Mumford, pastor of the South London Vineyard church, made a brief holiday visit to the Toronto church. She had heard of the unusual manifestations that for four months had accompanied the refreshing wave of God's power as the news spread through the worldwide Vineyard fellowship grapevine. Feeling dry spiritually and in need of a season of refreshing, she attended the services and received what is known as "soaking prayer"—repeated or extended prayer. Ellie Mumford was overcome by the "blessing" and refilled with the Holy Spirit and a divine expectancy that this was the beginning of a new move of the Spirit.

On returning to London, she shared her experiences with her friends on the staff of HTB. In a meeting, as she began to recount her experiences, the Holy Spirit fell on the members of the staff. Each one fell to the floor overcome by a sense of the presence of the Lord. They also began to laugh uncontrollably. After several hours the church secretary thought she had better phone the minister in charge.

Sandy Millar, vicar of Holy Trinity, was attending a meeting of the Evangelical Alliance elsewhere in London. He was summoned from that meeting to an "urgent" phone call.

"I just thought you should know," the secretary told him. "The entire staff of the church has been slain in the Spirit and is lying on the carpet. They are all laughing."

Sandy did not want to let on to his evangelical colleagues, who were within earshot and concerned about his urgent phone call. "Is that a good thing?"

"It's a wonderful thing."

"Well, if it's so wonderful, what are you doing on the phone?"

"I crawled," she replied.

The following Sunday in the morning and evening services, Ellie Mumford shared her testimony with the congregation of Holy Trinity, Brompton, about receiving the "blessing" in Toronto. The same signs and wonders accompanying the Toronto Blessing began to occur that very day among the parishioners of HTB.

Throughout the summer of 1994, queues of people outside the church before every service attracted the attention of Fleet Street, the seat of the British press. It had been a long time since people had to line up and get assigned tickets for available seats for any event in Britain besides a rock concert. And for church? Out of curiosity journalists began to attend services. Every newspaper tabloid carried stories of the outbreak of revival. The press soon dubbed the unusual phenomenon "the Toronto Blessing."

Before the outpouring at HTB, similar signs and wonders had occurred randomly in several other places in Britain. But HTB, perhaps because of its influence in London, became a center of the renewal that affected thousands of Anglican parishes and other churches in England. The revival in Sunderland, for example, now one of Britain's centers of renewal that holds meetings six nights a week, traces its renewal to the day the pastor of the Assembly of God church there, Ken Gott, went to HTB and was touched by the power of the Holy Spirit.

The influence of the renewal broadened beyond the scope of the Vineyard fellowships and into the mainstream of spiritual life in England. To date more than six thousand churches there from various denominations have been renewed by the "blessing." Many attribute the spreading fire to a unity of the Holy Spirit among churches in Great Britain—a unity that does not yet exist in America. The renewal in Britain is now at revival proportions and is accompanied by the beginnings of an increase in healings and an ingathering of the lost.

What is happening in the U.K. should give us faith for America—a prophetic portent of things to come if we open our arms to the new blessing God is pouring out.

Earmarks of the Blessing

Since the renewal with its accompanying signs has broken out in churches all over the world, we can recognize earmarks of what has become known as the Toronto Blessing.

"Carriers"

The wave of the Holy Spirit's power in this renewal is bringing to the thirsty a long-awaited drink of living water. Those who have been affected throughout the world have begun to unify around a renewed awareness of the heavenly Father's personal touch on their lives and a deeper intimacy with the Lord Jesus Christ. But although the blessing seems to be falling on some congregations sovereignly, the majority have been touched by someone who can trace the blessing back to prayer with someone who has been touched in Toronto, or to the evangelistic meetings of Rodney Howard-Browne, a South African evangelist.

The blessing is transmitted through yielded vessels by the laying on of hands in prayer. The person who transmits the blessing is usually open to receiving more of the Lord's presence in his or her life. Many of those who seemingly transmit the blessing, however, are "carriers" who have never experienced any outward manifestation themselves.

The term *carrier* may have originated with Stuart Bell, leader of New Life Fellowship in Lincoln, England. Stuart heads the Ground Level team, a stream of more than forty churches in Britain that sponsor the annual Grapevine conference, a camp meeting each summer of more than five thousand people. Stuart traces his experience to the day Dr. R. T. Kendall, pastor of Westminster Chapel in London, the famed evangelical pulpit, came to his church to speak.

Dr. Kendall appeared delighted to be invited to speak in a charismatic church and urged Stuart, at the close of the day of meetings, to open the altar for prayer. He encouraged the Lincoln church to be free to close the meeting as they saw fit. He had heard of the renewal and been prayed for himself, although nothing external had happened.

Later, over dinner, Dr. Kendall expressed his dismay at not receiving any outward sign.

Stuart, responding with concern, heard himself blurt out, "Well, we ought not to rely on our feelings. . . ." Then, with fear and trembling: "Perhaps you are a 'carrier' of the blessing?"

Later, before he left, Dr. Kendall prayed for those gathered in Stuart's office. Then he said, "If anything unusual happens to any of you within the next 24 hours, let me know."

The next day Stuart was scheduled to speak at two churches. The first was Ichthus, pastored by Roger Forster. The church had been holding meetings for a week already; people were being blessed and touched by the Holy Spirit's power. Stuart relates what happened next:

> Suddenly there was a sense that the spiritual climate in the room was rising. Roger asked me to pray for him. About halfway through my prayer, I was taken totally by surprise as Roger and I were knocked to the floor for about twenty minutes. I personally felt the power and love of God like "warm waves" passing over me. There were laughter, tears, confession of sin, humbleness, brokenness, and we had the privilege of being in what turned out to be about five hours of the very evident blessing of God upon our lives. . . .

Stuart went on to speak at the evening meeting of the Baptist church in Newark. At the end, after he had shared in a low-key manner, the leaders asked if he would pray for them before leaving. The power of God fell again, moving the leaders to laughter. The result: a deep work of the Holy Spirit in their lives.

Stuart notified Dr. Kendall immediately by mail of the extraordinary events that had occurred within 24 hours of the prayer with him in Stuart's office. To which Dr. Kendall sent a short reply: "Wow!"

The "spreadable" quality of this outpouring is an earmark of real revival. It belongs not to one denomination or fellowship, but to the Body of Christ.

Ordinary People

Nor is the renewal centered around any personality. While many have been newly filled with the Holy Spirit at the evangelistic meetings of Rodney Howard-Browne, the South African evangelist, the renewal is not limited to meetings where he is present. In fact, a new day has dawned on the Body of Christ.

On the Day of Pentecost, the Lord fulfilled Moses' prophecy in Numbers 11:29: "Would that all the LORD's people were prophets, that the LORD would put His Spirit upon them!" On Pentecost the Holy Spirit was made available to everyone who would trust Jesus as Savior and Lord. Throughout the centuries, history has recorded isolated instances of blessing beyond salvation for the hungry and thirsty, but not until the Azusa Street revival in Los Angeles in 1906–1909 did the Holy Spirit begin to be poured out corporately with signs and wonders, similar to those on Pentecost.

Throughout fresh waves of revival in this century, we have seen a gradual increase in the outpouring of the Holy Spirit, accompanied by speaking in tongues, prophecy and the other "sign" gifts of 1 Corinthians 12. The charismatic renewal—which started in 1959 with Dennis Bennett and other Episcopalians in California, and which multiplied in 1967 with an outpouring on a Catholic prayer retreat at Duquesne University—spread the Pentecostal blessing throughout hungry churches in mainline denominations. Since then new denominations and unaffiliated churches have sprung up as a direct result of this outpouring.

During the charismatic renewal, an experience subsequent to conversion known as the baptism in the Holy Spirit spread through the prayers of not only clergy but ordinary people touched by the Spirit's power. It was the dawning of a day in which we realized that the Holy Spirit is no respecter of persons, but will use any surrendered believer to transmit His blessings.

The Toronto Airport Christian Fellowship, because it was organized in the Vineyard model established by John Wimber, had already trained prayer teams to minister to those who answered the altar call in their services. When the Holy Spirit fell on January 20, 1994, the ministry of the prayer team became vital to the spreading of the blessing. As hungry seekers began to attend the meetings, prayer teams of ordinary Christians (with extraordinary commitments to the Lord) found themselves ministering literally to the world.

The prayer ministry of ordinary people and the practice of rotating speakers at the Toronto meetings, using local pastors to fill the pulpit, gave a nameless, faceless quality to the renewal. These practices de-emphasize the necessity for one revivalist to pray for those seeking prayer and make it possible for the anointing to be distributed through regular folks willing to allow God to use them. Perhaps these wise decisions are two of the factors that have perpetuated the renewal in Pastor Arnott's congregation and encouraged the worldwide spread of the blessing to the literal ends of the earth.

They have also encouraged another aspect that sets this renewal apart from others.

Soaking Prayer

Instead of receiving the entire benefit of the current renewal in one experience, those affected most deeply testify that the Holy Spirit's presence within them and work through them grow stronger as a result of repeated prayer.

During this new renewal, the blessing is spreading in churches and home prayer groups through the practice of "soaking prayer." The church in Toronto began to notice early on that those who surrender to prayer repeatedly begin to experience an increasingly powerful touch in their lives. Some who receive little initially begin to experience more, the more often they receive prayer. It is as though the dry ground is saturated through repeated waterings of the Holy Spirit.

Because many have seen visions about life-giving water, the metaphor of the revival quickly became "the river." It was as though the seekers had been thirsty and had found God's presence like a river flowing through a desert. As they submerged themselves continuously in the river, they became aware that their passion for Jesus was being renewed. In the same way that a river restores a desert, the river of renewal has been refreshing the dry lives of God's people. Their desire to share Him with others has begun to flow and they are constantly thirsty for more of Him.

Visions and Dreams

One of the unusual aspects of this visitation is that those under the influence of the Holy Spirit actually see visions—mental illustrations—similar to people of Bible times. Some have seen pictures of the deep workings of the Holy Spirit to heal their bruised emotions. Young men and women in our congregation have received visions of the heavenly Father demonstrating His affection for them. Others have seen visions concerning the coming harvest, the deepening river and the awakening of the Church.

The charismatic renewal of the 1960s and '70s saw an increase of such prophetic activity, but the prophetic dimension poured out on believers of all ages and from many countries and walks of life has seen a dramatic increase. In fact, visions have become so common that their frequency is almost taken for granted. The power of the Holy Spirit that accompanies the visions, bringing release from bondage and a sense of divine expectation, testifies to the fruit of them.

In October 1994, the month before Bill and I visited Toronto, we made a two-week trip to England and stayed with our friends Kevin and Pam Swadling, now directors of Christ for the Nations, United Kingdom. They, like other friends, told us of the river that had washed through their fellowship. We remained adamant that such a fad meandering through the Church would soon die out and expose the fact that the "revival" had been a counterfeit.

During the Sunday morning service at their church, Chichester Christian Fellowship, the congregation prayed for us. One of the members of the congregation, although she knew nothing about us, said during that prayer time, "You have been waiting on God for years. Everything you've been waiting on God for is just behind a curtain, and He is about to part the curtain."

I did not doubt that this message was from God, but was in such a state of dryness that I was tired of hearing prophecies. I wanted a day of fulfillment.

That evening a contingent of people from the church who had just returned from the Airport Fellowship gave their testimonies. Still skeptical, Bill and I allowed them to pray for us. Nothing happened. At least, nothing we noticed then.

A week later we were in Madrid visiting our friends Mary and Elliott Tepper. I dreamed one night that I was in a restaurant with Bill, when I spotted at the next table a healing evangelist and his wife. I went over to their table and began to pour out my heart, telling them how badly we needed to see revival.

Suddenly the countenances of the couple changed and became that of two men. One of the men interrupted me. "Have I not promised you times of refreshing from the Lord?"

When those words left his mouth, they became alive inside of me. I do not know how else to say it. And in the dream I felt myself overcome by the Holy Spirit's presence as though I had been "slain in the Spirit"—although I had never had that experience in my life.

The next morning I awoke with a profound awareness of the presence of God that I had not felt in years. All that day and the next, I had a sense of His presence, and the beginnings of a revival of hope in my heart. I did not realize it, but the river was beginning to lap at my feet. I was beginning to thirst for more of the Lord's presence and was willing to do anything to find Him again.

Within a few days I began to "see" clear pictures in my mind describing the Lord's intentions for this renewal in my own life, in the life of our congregation and in the Body of Christ.

Joel prophesied:

> "And it will come about after this that I will pour out My Spirit on all mankind; and your sons and your daughters will prophesy, your old men will dream dreams, your young men will see visions. And even on the male and female servants I will pour out My Spirit in those days."
>
> Joel 2:28–29

A few weeks after the renewal began in our congregation, I saw in my mind's eye, while we were praying, the Lord Jesus standing in a river that was chest-deep. He was laughing and enjoying Himself. People were gathering at the bank and sticking their toes gingerly into the water. As they did so, the Lord would grab them by the ankles and yank them into the river. He said, "I've been looking forward to the day of visitation more than you have!"

Seeing this picture of the Lord's great pleasure brought me a sense of rest concerning the renewal. Having struggled with a deep-seated fear of abandonment, I have often projected it into a fear of abandonment by my heavenly Father. I have been anxious concerning His willingness to revive the Church and to bless me with this outpouring. I have also experienced a false pressure to "earn" the blessing. This one picture provided a giant step in my emotional healing and a great encouragement to others struggling with the Lord's willingness to bless.

This gracious understanding of the Lord's overwhelming desire to bless and revive the Church reveals two other aspects of this current outpouring.

Intercession

The disappointed hearts of many Christians have quenched their desire to pray. When faith is at a low ebb, it is difficult to pray with expectation. I have already said that Christians in that condition cannot pray for revival. But one of the wonderful aspects of this renewal is the accompanying longing for a deeper intimacy with the Lord. This anointing impresses the believer with the personal concern of the Lord for his or her life, which increases his desire to pray both corporately and privately. Some confess to an ongoing communion with the Lord throughout the day—even a consumption with the desire to get alone with the Lord and worship Him.

And in this renewal, intercession has taken on a new dimension. Many believers, rather than approach the Lord with a set of requests—for example, the salvation of specific loved ones or the outpouring of God over countries and cities—now begin times of corporate prayer by asking the Lord to show them what to pray for. As the group waits on Him, they are amazed to find themselves impressed by a thread of concern, by way of a vision or impression on the mind or certain phrases or passages of Scripture that draw their attention to the Lord's concerns rather than their own. This new way to pray encourages believers that they are hearing from God the same things that others are hearing.

One Friday night at the Church of the Risen Saviour, as a wedding rehearsal was taking place in the sanctuary, we were waiting on the Lord, asking Him how to pray. After several minutes, several shared that the Lord was telling them to pray for healings in the congregation. Two women actually "saw" the same vision without conferring about it previously. We began to pray about this vision. Suddenly the Lord filled our mouths with laughter. For several minutes we laughed in what we knew was victory. Later we learned that some in the wedding party rehearsing in the sanctuary wanted to call off the rehearsal and come to the intercessory prayer meeting!—a far cry from the days when no one wanted to intercede because intercession seemed to be a fruitless, vague pursuit full of morose appeals to God for things we did not believe would happen anyway.

Love for the Scriptures

Prayer has increased people's hunger for God's Word. Believers who a year ago were hard-pressed to read Scripture in a printed, daily devotional guide are beginning to linger over the Bible, finding it full of personal, intimate messages.

One of the first manifestations I noticed after several weeks of "soaking prayer" came one night as I went to bed and glimpsed my Bible on the nightstand. I reached for it and realized that for the first time in several years, I was hungry for it. After several years of dutiful reading only to get a sermon, I was surprised that my affection for the Word of God had returned. The thought of reading it actually excited me.

After the Great Awakening, Jonathan Edwards wrote,

> While God was so remarkably present amongst us by his Spirit, there was no book so delightful as the Bible. . . . Some, by reason of their love to God's word, at times have been wonderfully delighted and affected at the sight of a Bible. . . .
>
> *A Narrative of Surprising Conversions*, p. 47

Revival seems to have that effect on everyone, regardless of the era in which they live. But there are other remarkable aspects of the Toronto Blessing.

Physical Manifestations

As in other revivals in past centuries and in the recent past, the invasion of God's power has brought about unusual phenomena in the form of physical manifestations. Because accounts of these phenomena have often been edited out of modern versions of early revival literature, the Christian today is left with the impression that revival invaded the Church in past times unobtrusively. But this is not true.

The phenomena that accompany today's outpouring are similar in nature but much more widespread, reaching worldwide proportions. They are responsible (as in the past) not only for drawing attention to the new thing God is doing but also for engendering criticism and providing a stumblingblock to those who want a "clean" revival.

Let's look now at these manifestations.

4

Why Can't We Have Revival without Those Manifestations?

Two days after Bill and I returned from Toronto, I became angry, perhaps because all I had seen was so new. I did not understand why God would make all those people laugh—including me. So I began to reevaluate everything, thinking perhaps I had been caught up in the emotion of the moment. *Why, I wondered, can't we just have revival without all those crazy manifestations?*

"If this is God," I told my husband, "why doesn't He move on someone in our church and make them apologize for some of the pain they've caused us in the last twenty years?"

I still was looking for the sweeping move of repentance that always accompanies revival.

Two hours later the doorbell on our back porch rang. Standing at the door was Jennie Blackham.

Jennie and her husband, Paul, had met at our church. Bill had performed their wedding ceremony ten years before. But the time since had been difficult for them. Although they both have college degrees, Paul had been unable to find a job since financial problems had forced them to leave Bible college. Jennie had suffered two miscarriages, and the weight of so much unresolved emotional pain had driven them to the brink of despair. We watched them sink under the weight without knowing how to do anything except pray for them and accept them, problems and all.

Finally Paul and Jennie had decided they needed another church setting. Bill and I did not try to stand in their way. We have found it best through the years to bless people as they go. But Jennie had much in her heart that she felt she needed to express.

After they left our church, I received a long letter from Jennie. It came on a day that was already a low point for me. I was struggling with my own emotional pain. The words of the letter stung. I managed to pull myself together, and Bill and I sent them a card and invited them back to visit anytime they wanted to.

Now here she was at the back door. But in place of the dark expression we had become accustomed to, her face was glowing. She was holding a peace offering—a wool suit, my colors.

In shock I invited her in. She wanted to talk to me about what had happened to her.

After they had left our congregation, Jennie said, they had begun visiting another church whose pastor had been to Toronto. During an altar call she had gone up for prayer. When the pastor touched her forehead, she had fallen to the carpet and laughed hysterically for 45 minutes as the Lord pulled out a deeply rooted plug of emotional pain.

Jennie did not have to tell me she was different. In place of despair, I saw hope. In a few moments the Lord had been able to touch her in a way that hundreds of our sermons and teachings had not.

Jennie visited awhile and left. I cried for several hours. It was as though Jesus had been so close to me that He had listened in on my angry outburst earlier. He had heard it as a prayer and answered it immediately.

Paul and Jennie are back. Paul is one of our worship leaders. Jennie is on the prayer ministry team. Their situation has not changed all that much, but they are facing things full of the Holy Spirit now. For nearly a year they have been soaked in prayer at every service, with some unusually strong manifestations accompanying each touch of the Lord. Their countenances still glow. Jennie testified recently about how much joy it gives her to pray for people as a member of the prayer team. "I was born to pray for people!" she exults.

The divine Plumber had started His repairs, this time using equipment I had never heard of—laughter—to bring about repentance and reconciliation. The incident with Jennie and Paul was the sign I needed to embrace fully what God is doing today.

What *is* God doing today?

God Invading Our Boundaries

I used to believe God would not do anything in a church service to make me feel uncomfortable. I wanted to hear the rushing, mighty wind as they did on Pentecost, so long as it did not mess up my hair! Emotional displays have always unnerved me—unless, of course, they are coming from me. I know how far I will let myself go; I do not know how far *other* people will go. But sometimes God offends us to show us attitudes that are in His way. I have heard a saying: "God will offend your mind to reveal what's in your heart."

But why do we feel uncomfortable?

Civilized human beings have a fear of shaming ourselves. To behave outside the bounds of propriety, to violate the rules, may bring about disapproval from others and result in rejection. Many of those rules have been instilled in us by our parents, who wanted us to learn how to behave so that we might be accepted socially and, for heaven's sake, not embarrass them! As adults we want to be in settings where things will not happen that embarrass us or make us feel ashamed.

But the sense of shame becomes false when we feel ashamed over what God is doing. Let the Lord expose your false sense of shame and replace it with a willingness to be broken enough to allow Him room to move, even though the emotional responses of others to His power may embarrass you a little. Believe me, the fruit is worth it. And you will come to love God better when He is out of control—*your* control!

The preaching of eighteenth-century evangelist John Wesley awakened surprisingly emotional responses in his listeners, for which he was criticized widely. From his journal for June 15, 1739:

> Many of those that heard began to call upon God with strong cries and tears. Some sunk down, and there remained no strength in them; others exceedingly trembled and quaked: some were torn with a kind of convulsive motion in every part of their bodies, and that so violently, that often four or five persons could not hold one of them. . . . I immediately prayed, that God would not suffer those who were weak to be offended. But one woman was offended greatly; being sure they might help it if they would;—no one should persuade her to the contrary; and was got three or four yards, when she also dropped down in as violent an agony as the rest.
>
> *The Works of John Wesley*
> (Baker, 1991), p. 204

Let's examine the ministry of Jesus to see if He was sensitive to what others might think about what He said and did.

The Embarrassing Jesus

Not long into the ministry of the Lord Jesus, the disciples realized that to follow Him meant they had to bear with the unusual and unexpected. In fact, Peter wrote in his epistle that "to you who believe, He is precious; but to those who are disobedient, . . . 'a stone of stumbling and a rock of offense'" (1 Peter 2:7–8, NKJV).

Jesus did not seem to care what anyone thought when He talked with a Samaritan woman at the well; nor what the host of a banquet in Jesus' honor thought when He received the worship of an adulterous woman who invaded the formal affair; nor what the Gerasenes thought when Jesus commanded the legion of demons to go into the herd of pigs; nor what religious people thought about His failure to observe Jewish traditions that had risen up around the Law of Moses, such as eating with unwashed hands. He cared more about the needy than about human beings' definition of the Sabbath.

Jesus purposely said things He knew would offend. "Unless you eat the flesh of the Son of Man and drink His blood," He declared in the synagogue, "you have no life in yourselves" (John 6:53). He did not bother to explain it; He just let it fall. Multitudes were so offended that they stopped following Him. On another day Jesus cried out at one of the most solemn moments of a Temple ceremony in front of a huge crowd, "If any man is thirsty, let him come to Me and drink" (John 7:37). On at least two occasions He wept in front of others.

I do not know if you want me to continue. There is plenty more. But in all these things Jesus was testing the love and loyalty of hearers and followers alike. He was invading manmade boundaries of religiosity and propriety that stood in God's way.

Through these examples I am not giving permission to the overzealous believer to interrupt services without concern for spiritual authority in the local church. I *am* asking Christian leaders to take a long, hard look at their own traditions and whatever makes them feel uncomfortable. Ask yourself this question before you rule out this renewal or any particular manifestation: *What if it is God?*

Bill and I have learned to allow emotional demonstrations, but we reserve the authority as pastors to ask people what is going on in their hearts. If a manifestation is truly Christ-centered, you will see evidence of His ministry to them, a new freedom, a sense of His presence, a godly desire being restored, a healing that glorifies Him.

One of the early questions I needed an answer to was, Are these things scriptural? We need to ask, too, if particular manifestations are in keeping with the Holy Spirit behind the Word. After all, Paul wrote, "The letter kills, but the Spirit gives life" (2 Corinthians 3:6). It is possible to interpret Scripture so rigidly that we miss what God is doing.

Before we look at some manifestations themselves, let's look at some scriptural evidence for reasons God uses signs and wonders.

Why Signs and Wonders?

Whenever God begins a new season, He usually gives us a series of signs. If we are watching for Him, we will see these as signals that the old day is passing and a new day in God is dawning.

Just before Jesus was born, the Lord broke a four-hundred-year prophetic silence in Israel by sending an angel to Zacharias, the father of John the Baptist. The angelic visitation frightened him. But Gabriel tried to put Zacharias' fears to rest and give him a message he had waited for personally and ministerially all his life. He and his barren wife, Elizabeth, would have a child who would be the prophet to usher in the long-awaited Messiah. Zacharias was so surprised and frightened that he did not fully believe it.

We may want to criticize Zacharias for his unbelief, but could *you* accept something today unquestioningly that had not happened to anyone since the 1500s or even since Bible times? By Zacharias' day, religious people had adopted (as some have today) a doctrine of cessationism—the idea that miracles are only for Bible times.

The message of the angel Gabriel was the first in a series of visitations to ordinary people. Apparently there was no one God wanted to use as a prophet. Or perhaps, at this most special moment in human history, the Lord simply preferred an angel. In any case, these supernatural occurrences signaled a break between the Old and New Covenants, the day of Messiah's coming to Israel.

The ministry of Jesus was full of signs and wonders—statements He made that fulfilled prophecy and miraculous occurrences that drew attention to the fact that He was more than a prophet; He was the Son of God.

After Jesus died on the cross, rose from the dead and ascended into heaven, He sent the Holy Spirit to mediate God's activity on earth. But the Spirit did not sneak up on human beings without warning. His coming was signaled by another wave of signs and wonders.

On the Day of Pentecost, the Holy Spirit fell on the waiting 120 believers with the sound of a forceful wind that filled not only the room where they were sitting but the entire house (see Acts 2).

The advent of the third Person of the Trinity falling on the disciples in power caused manifestations that made other people wonder. Flames of fire hovered over the believers' heads and they began to speak in languages they had not learned—something that had never happened in human history. When Peter preached his famous message on the Day of Pentecost, enabled by the Holy Spirit to speak to people from other places and cultures, several thousand were added to the Church within the next few days.

Later this manifestation was given to many others who received the Holy Spirit (see Acts 10, 11, 19). We know that tongues were given to the apostle Paul and many other Christians, because Paul instructed them on the proper use of praying with the spirit as opposed to praying with the mind, and on the public manifestation of tongues with interpretation in a meeting (see 1 Corinthians 14). Paul wanted the manifestations of the Holy Spirit's power to bring glory to Jesus Christ. In those early days of the Church, "everyone kept feeling a sense of awe; and many wonders and signs were taking place through the apostles" (Acts 2:43).

Signs and wonders do produce awe. And apparently in this case they were too numerous to mention. But what possible glory can God receive from some of the manifestations in this twentieth-century renewal?

At first this question plagued me. But our ways are not God's ways. Sometimes in the Church, we who know Jesus lose our awe of Him. Faith ebbs and we revert to "maintenance mode." But the lost are seldom attracted to a church that is in maintenance mode.

So what must God do in order to refresh and renew those who have already accepted Jesus and have been walking in the power of the Holy Spirit? What if God's people have been disillusioned with the miraculous and have lost faith in His willingness to do the impossible? Although some might say He should not do anything, God is full of mercy and love. He knows our weak frames and longs to wash our feet again with a refreshing sense of His presence.

That is one of the chief purposes of revival: to renew the saints in their faith. God must get the attention of Christians who are used to business as usual at church. Is it possible that He would choose to invade our lives with a new wave of the power of the Holy Spirit and use different signs and wonders that cause us to investigate, question and be in awe of His sovereign majesty and ability to bowl us over?

Signs and wonders born of the Holy Spirit always glorify Jesus in some way. Jesus Himself warned of other "great signs and wonders" that will draw attention to false prophets who will "mislead, if possible, even the elect" (Matthew 24:24). Signs and wonders alone, then, do not signify the work of the Holy Spirit. Remember the signs performed by the magicians in Pharaoh's court alongside those performed by Moses and Aaron. If, on the other hand, we see a church being infused with a hunger for God and deep love for Jesus Christ, we may assume that God Himself is somewhere behind the manifestations.

Jonathan Edwards faced the same challenges during the Great Awakening in 1735 that we face today. "There never yet was any great manifestation that God made of Himself to the world," wrote Edwards in his essay "Distinguishing Marks of the Work of the Spirit of God," his defense of the revival, "without many difficulties attending it" (*Edwards on Revival,* p. 133). During Edwards' meetings, many were overcome by "tears, trembling, groans, loud outcries, agonies of body, or the failing of bodily strength." Edwards also observed that the presence of these manifestations did not indicate that the work was from God or not from God. Rather, he detailed numerous ways to discern the presence of the Holy Spirit in the wake of such things. One of the chief evidences to Edwards was love:

> Therefore, when the spirit that is at work amongst the people . . . brings many of them to high and exalting thoughts of the Divine Being, and his glorious perfections; and works in them an admiring, delightful sense of the excellency of Jesus Christ; representing him as the chief among ten thousand, and altogether lovely, and makes him precious to the soul; winning and drawing the heart with those motives and incitements to love . . . the wonderful free love of God in

giving His only-begotten Son to die for us, and the wonderful dying love of Christ to us who had no love to Him but were his enemies . . . it must needs be the Spirit of God. . . .

p. 116

Physical Manifestations

What, then, are some of the phenomena taking place in today's revival? And is there scriptural or historical precedent?

Groanings Too Deep for Words

On my first trip to Toronto, at the end of the service on the first night, I could only sit and watch during the prayer time. Hundreds of people lay on their backs on the floor. Some were crying out, others were laughing, some were shouting, even roaring. I did not know what to make of it. In fact, it took me 24 hours to summon the courage to seek prayer myself, for fear I would be among those making a public display. I could not understand why such a large group of people, most of them pastors, would be affected like this.

Once I began to receive prayer myself, however, the Lord recalled this Scripture from my memory:

> . . . We ourselves, having the first fruits of the Spirit, even we ourselves groan within ourselves, waiting eagerly for our adoption as sons, the redemption of our body. . . . And in the same way the Spirit also helps our weakness; for we do not know how to pray as we should, but the Spirit Himself intercedes for us with groanings too deep for words.
>
> Romans 8:23, 26

Although we think we have a framework for "groaning" in intercessory prayer—as the wordless prayer that cannot be articulated—suppose there is more to it than that? Suppose the infinite God invades a human spirit with such a vast display of love and power that the person can only cry out?

Some believers find themselves groaning as a woman giving birth. Sometimes such groaning is associated with intercession or with the "birthing" of a message from God, a vision or a ministry.

59

Examining the fruit (as Jonathan Edwards recommended) will help those of us who are used to seeing such gut-wrenching manifestations only when demons are being cast out. Early in the renewal, in fact, we were certain that most of those on the floor were crying out because they were receiving deliverance. Indeed, some of these may be receiving a sovereign releasing touch from the Lord. When Bill and I questioned most of them later, however, we discovered that the joy of God's presence was so overwhelming that they could only cry out in joy. Others were seeing visions with coordinating sounds.

Groaning may take many different forms. One of the most unusual to date is roaring—a phenomenon John Wesley encountered. From his journal entry for April 17, 1739:

> Soon after, two other persons (well known in this place, as labouring to live in all good conscience towards all men) were seized with strong pain, and constrained to "roar for the disquietness of their heart." But it was not long before they likewise burst forth into praise to God their Saviour.

Sue Swackhamer, one of the members of the worship team at Church of the Risen Saviour, is a friendly, joyful person, always affirming and loving. One day as she was receiving prayer lying on the carpet at the altar, she sensed a roar welling up within her. Gentle, friendly Sue began to roar so loudly that we were startled.

During the next service she testified that while she was on the floor, the Holy Spirit showed her some serious situations involving people in her life she had to confront. She is not a confronter. In fact, she tends to avoid confrontation at all costs. But the Lord was showing Sue that He would give her the authority and power. And at that moment she began to roar.

Since then the Lord has given her unprecedented boldness to speak to co-workers and friends about Jesus, as well as to prophesy.

During one of our special renewal weekends, Stuart Bell, pastor of New Life Fellowship in Lincoln, England, and a leader in the so-called "new" church movement in Britain, preached a message from

Amos 1:2: "The Lord roars from Zion. . . ." His point was that the lion roars whenever injustice prevails in the land.

During a meeting in England, while Stuart was receiving prayer and soaking in the Lord's presence, he realized two teenagers were roaring over him. Later he heard them crying out in deep agony of soul, "The poor, the poor, the poor. . . ." Earlier the Lord had been interceding through them with groanings too deep for words, and now was giving words to accompany their profound burden. Indeed, the lives of these two young men do bear out an increased concern for the poor.

As we examine the Scriptures, we see that many of the prophets accompanied and reinforced their prophetic themes with prophetic acts. Moses, Isaiah, Jeremiah, Ezekiel, Hosea and others all acted out their prophecies. Moses struck the rock. Isaiah went naked and barefoot for three years. Jeremiah bought a field. Ezekiel lay on his side for a full year. Hosea, under the instruction of the Lord (don't try this at home!), married a prostitute. Amos wrote, "A lion has roared! Who will not fear? The Lord GOD has spoken! Who can but prophesy?" (3:8).

From months of observation, I have come to believe that a new prophetic anointing is coming to enable the Church to function in greater authority. I am seeing an impartation of divine courage to the fainthearted to proclaim the Gospel.

If God has chosen the weak and foolish things to confound the wise (see 1 Corinthians 1:27, KJV), there will be times He uses our mouths and causes us to break out of our inhibitions. Some church auditoriums may literally be turned into prophetic schools full of Christians being acted upon so powerfully that they go forth courageously to speak in love anything God wants them to say that will draw the lost into a loving relationship with their heavenly Father.

Laughter

A year ago our daughter, Sarah, was afraid to speak to anyone about salvation. Last summer while home from college, Sarah began to receive prayer at the altar at every service. She became filled with the Holy Spirit, the love of God and concern for the soul of a young man who worked across the hall from her in her summer job at the mall. One day she walked to the mall and spent two hours talking to him about the unfailing love of Jesus Christ, the joy she had found and his need to accept Jesus as Lord and Savior. The young man surrendered his heart to Christ that evening.

The manifestation Sarah had been experiencing most frequently was "holy laughter."

The first time I heard this manifestation, I was convinced that those giving themselves over to it were attempting to stir themselves up. I have no doubt this *is* happening to some. There is evidence in Scripture, however, for laughter on the part of God and on the parts of people being acted on by God.

The psalmist sang,

> When the Lord brought back the captive ones of Zion, we were like those who dream. Then our mouth was filled with laughter, and our tongue with joyful shouting. . . . Those who sow in tears shall reap with joyful shouting.
>
> Psalm 126:1–2, 5

Holy laughter is a release of great joy over the saving and delivering work of God. It follows a long period of captivity and represents a sign of victory. The righteous laugh at the evil man in Psalm 52:6 for that reason. And before the Lord judges His enemies, He laughs at them in Psalm 2:4 and 37:12–13. The writer of Ecclesiastes says there is "a time to weep, and a time to laugh" (3:4). Jesus promised those who weep now that "you shall laugh" (Luke 6:21).

When Abraham was promised by God that within a year his son would be born, Abraham fell to the ground and laughed. Sarah also laughed in her tent and lied to the angel about having done so. When Isaac was born, Sarah said, "God has made me laugh, so that all who hear will laugh with me" (Genesis 21:6, NKJV). When God removed the curse of barrenness from Abraham and Sarah and fulfilled His promises to them, He put laughter in their mouths as well as in their arms. The name *Isaac* means "laughter."

The entrance of God's only begotten Son into the barren life of the oppressed should cause laughter and rejoicing, too.

Today we are seeing God once again putting laughter into the mouths of the oppressed and freeing them from depression and grief. Allowing the manifestation (like the others) seems to strengthen the sense of God's presence, and to quench it seems to diminish it.

Linda Heron is a schoolteacher with a master's degree and gentle demeanor. She seldom does anything to draw attention to herself but serves the Lord contentedly in the background. So we were all amazed the night that Linda, who had been sitting at the front of the church watching others receive prayer, suddenly fell over in her seat convulsed with laughter. She laughed for more than an hour. Her husband, Tom, had to help her to the car. We only hoped she would not be arrested for disturbing the peace! Forty-five minutes after she left the church, I got a call in my office. It was Linda, still in paroxysms of laughter. I punched the speaker button on the phone so the others in the office could hear her. We could not help laughing, too.

The reason Linda phoned was that, once home, she had opened her diary to record the incident and happened to notice the date at the top of the page. It was five years ago on that date that her younger sister had died after suffering terribly with cancer. Through gasps between laughs, Linda managed to say on the phone that the Lord had told her He was lifting her burden of grief and that she would never grieve that loss again.

The Lord had also directed Linda to the story of the Prodigal Son. She had worried for five years about the eternal destiny of her sister and did not know if she had made a commitment to Jesus Christ. Now Linda's eyes fell on a verse: "For this my son was dead and is alive again; he was lost and is found" (Luke 15:24, NKJV). It was God's way of letting her know that her sister was home, safe in the arms of her heavenly Father.

The Lord broke Linda's yoke of heaviness and grief by putting laughter in her mouth as a sign and wonder that a new day was dawning—a day of deliverance from the overwhelming sadness that had weighed down her heart.

In previous revivals God put laughter in the mouths of many He filled with the Holy Spirit. Jonathan Edwards and John Wesley were both overcome with holy laughter. In his book *Revival* (Whitaker House, 1983), Winkie Pratney quotes a newspaper account of the Welsh revival meetings with Evan Roberts:

> It may be observed that the dominant note of the revival was prayer and praise. Another striking fact was the joyous and radiant happiness of the evangelist. It has been remarked that the very essence of Roberts' campaign was mirth. To the rank and file of church ministers, this was his most incomprehensible quality. They had always regarded religion as something iron-bound, severe, even terrible. Evan Roberts smiled when he prayed, laughed when he preached. . . .
>
> p. 175

Why have we always linked holiness with solemnity? Is it perhaps because of the vision of the great white throne of judgment in Revelation 20? But those who love Jesus' appearing will not shrink from Him in fear. Heaven—where there will be no more tears, sorrow, crying or pain—will be filled with sounds of joy like nothing we have ever heard. As much as any earthly father loves to arrive home from a hard day at work to a home full of joyful, happy children ready to hug him, I believe the heavenly Father is putting laughter into our hearts and mouths to relieve us of sorrow and fill us with the Holy Spirit.

I further believe that the laughter we are seeing now is a sign from God that He is about to judge His enemies and bring great triumph to the Church as we gather in the harvest. The laughter seems to have a prophetic as well as healing quality. Proverbs 15:13 (NKJV) says, "A merry heart makes a cheerful countenance, but by sorrow of the heart the spirit is broken." In light of the heaviness and discouragement that have prevailed over the Church during the past decade, could the Lord be filling our mouths with laughter as a sign that a new day of miracles, release and joy is dawning?

"The Jerks"

Some believers—like the woman I heard testifying in Toronto, or like Haley, a young Englishwoman we will meet in chapter 5—feel their stomach muscles contracting involuntarily, causing them to "jerk." This phenomenon appeared in the revival meetings of Edwards, Wesley, Finney and many others, including the multidenominational Cane Ridge (Kentucky) revival of 1801, in which 25,000 were converted to Jesus Christ.

"Drunkenness"

Laughter can become so overwhelming and lengthy that it results in a state akin to drunkenness. There are also people who, when the Holy Spirit falls on them, become "drunk" almost instantly.

On the Day of Pentecost, something similar occurred to the believers on whom the Holy Spirit fell. The observers, drawn to the scene by the tongues and sounds of wind, asked what everyone today is asking: "Whatever could this mean?" (Acts 2:12, NKJV). Other bystanders began to accuse the disciples of being "full of new wine" (verse 13). But good old Peter set them straight: "These are not drunk, as you suppose . . ." (verse 15).

Why would onlookers charge that those who had received the Holy Spirit were drunk? Because something was happening visibly to the disciples besides speaking in other languages. No one is accused of being drunk because he or she is speaking a foreign language. It is reasonable to conjecture that the fullness of joy accompanying the infilling of the Holy Spirit produced in them a state resembling inebriation, perhaps accompanied by laughter or exuberance.

Paul knew about such fullness and advocated the experience for everyone:

> Be not drunk with wine, wherein is excess; but be filled with the Spirit; speaking to yourselves in psalms and hymns and spiritual songs, singing and making melody in your heart to the Lord.
>
> Ephesians 5:18–19, KJV

Have you ever seen television programs showing saloons in the old West? Invariably patrons got so drunk they laughed even at things that were not funny, ridiculing their own problems, singing loudly, crowing, shouting, dancing on tables. These are manifestations of drunkenness. Likewise, there is an overwhelming joy that floods the human soul on being filled with the Holy Spirit that may also, if intense enough, cause similar responses! Many of the more unusual vocal responses observed during this renewal may fall into this category.

Laughter is known to release endorphins into the body that actually give an individual a pervasive sense of well-being. Laughter is known to build up the body's ability to fight off disease. Psychologists have initiated a new field of study to explore the effects of laughter and other emotional states on the immune system. No wonder the Scripture encourages us to take advantage of this natural medicine for the soul and body!

Church, it is time to celebrate. Like Boaz in Ruth 3:7, the Lord Jesus may be celebrating the beginning of harvest time by causing the Body of Christ to be merry. He may want us, for a season preceding the final harvest, to lose our sense of balance and sense of direction; to cease striving, wailing and fasting, and celebrate a feast time to Him.

This generation needs to be strengthened with joy. Nehemiah put an end to the grieving of God's people over having ignored the words of the Law. Excessive sadness, he knew, would demoralize them. So he encouraged them to

> "Go your way, eat the fat, drink the sweet, and send portions to those for whom nothing is prepared; for this day is holy to our LORD. Do not sorrow, for the joy of the LORD is your strength." . . . And all the people went their way to eat and drink, to send portions and rejoice greatly, because they understood the words that were declared to them.
>
> Nehemiah 8:10, 12, NKJV

Paul told the Ephesians, in the admonition we just looked at, not only to be baptized with the Holy Spirit but to be filled continuously with the Spirit. Had they done it, perhaps they would not have left their first love and been reproved by Jesus (see Revelation 2:4).

Perhaps this newest renewal will leave a tradition of being filled with the Holy Spirit every day, or at least at every church service.

Resting in the Spirit

Perhaps the most common phenomenon is the vast numbers of those who fall to the floor under the influence of the Holy Spirit when they are receiving soaking prayer. This event has been seen in the Pentecostal and charismatic outpourings during this century and also in the ministries of several well-known healing evangelists.

During the Great Awakening, Jonathan Edwards observed "faintings," as he called them. Wesley, Whitefield and Finney also saw this phenomenon in their meetings. In this century it is commonly called "being slain the Spirit" or "going down under the power."

Jonathan Edwards, in "Distinguishing Marks of the Work of the Spirit of God," concerning the phenomenon during the Great Awakening, made several remarks about the numerous occasions of those falling.

> So it may easily be accounted for, that a true sense of the glorious excellency of the Lord Jesus Christ, and of His wonderful dying love, and the exercise of a truly spiritual love and joy, should be such as very much to overcome the bodily strength. We are all ready to own that no man can see God and live, and that it is but a very small part of that apprehension of the glory and the love of Christ which the saints enjoy in heaven, that our present frame can bear; therefore, it is not at all strange that God should sometimes give his saints such foretastes of heaven as to diminish their bodily strength.
>
> p. 92

Overcome by God

The Scriptures describe instances in which individuals were so overcome with the power of God's presence that they fell. Recall that Abraham "fell on his face" (Genesis 17:17) as he laughed about God's promise of a son when he was soon to be a hundred years old. Daniel, approached by "the glorious man," wrote that "no strength remained in me" (10:8, NKJV), and he lay with his face to the ground. The soldiers and officers who arrested Jesus in the Garden of Gethsemane were overcome by the power of the Holy Spirit as Jesus rose from the place of prayer, and they "fell to the ground" (John 18:6). The apostle John, exiled on the Isle of Patmos and receiving a vision of the victorious, exalted Christ, "fell at His feet as dead" (Revelation 1:17, NKJV). Saul of Tarsus, confronted by a vision of the Lord Jesus on the road to Damascus, "fell to the ground" (Acts 9:4), along with all the men with him (see Acts 26:14).

All of these seem to have fallen as a result of the powerful impact of the presence of God.

Honoring God

The Scriptures are also filled with examples of those who chose to fall as a means of humbling themselves to worship God or honor the impact of what was taking place before them.

Ezekiel "fell on [his] face" as he saw the visions of the four living creatures and "the appearance of the likeness of the glory of the LORD" (1:28). Jairus "fell at Jesus' feet" (Luke 8:41) when he implored the Lord to come to his house and heal his daughter. Peter "fell down at Jesus' knees" (Luke 5:8, NKJV) when he saw the miraculous catch of fish that provoked him to discipleship.

Both of these physical responses—falling under the loss of physical strength and dropping to the floor in worship—seem to be occurring during the renewal. Some fall as they sense a wave of power that is too difficult to resist. Others are yielding to the impact of the voice of God in their spirits or to the awe of a vision they are seeing. Some are choosing to surrender in the same way that others raise their hands.

What's the Good of It?

For a time I believed that the Holy Spirit knocked people unconscious for a short time. I was further confused to see people fainting and hopping back up, as though God took delight in seeing whether He could push a person over. I had also observed (as I have said) what seemed to be shoving, rocking, pushing or the use of other intimidating means to encourage people to fall. Seeing these things caused me to doubt the validity of the occurrence. Observing the widespread lack of fruit from these experiences had also convinced me they were either false or of little value. I wanted what was real, but believed the real to be so rare that only an isolated few would experience it.

During this renewal, however, I have observed resting in the Spirit as the most common external manifestation. Frequently those who fall remain on the floor under the influence of the Holy Spirit for periods of minutes to hours. Theologians and students of the revival have commented that to get up too soon is to shortchange a deep work of the Spirit. Unlike previous times, this phenomenon seems to be occurring widely to those who have previously scorned it or for other reasons never yielded to it.

Drs. Marie and Lowell Hoffman, clinical psychologists practicing in the Lehigh Valley in eastern Pennsylvania, have observed the tendency among those receiving prayer to want to be in a reclining position. The Hoffmans pointed out to me that Sigmund Freud, known as the father of modern psychology, commented on this fact of human nature in his observations of human psychological response. Human beings, he discovered, were most vulnerable when lying down. For this reason many psychiatrists today still have their patients lie on a couch as they receive counseling. It is no wonder that, as we are receiving inner healing, God may choose to put us into the same position.

Sometimes the person responding this way to the Holy Spirit's presence has the feeling of being acted on by the power of God that is greater than themselves. John Crane, pastor of Evangelistic Center Church, Kansas City, is more than six feet three inches tall and massive in build. As he received prayer in Toronto, he, too, fell as the Holy Spirit's presence swept over him. This had never happened to him before. As he lay on the floor, he asked, "Lord, is this scriptural?" Immediately a verse flashed across his mind: "He makes me lie down in green pastures" (Psalm 23:2)!

When sheep lie down in a pasture, they are enjoying a place of contentment and freedom from fear. Perhaps the Lord is placing many of His sheep, like John Crane, in this position to soothe and free them.

Some people want to know if someone should stand behind the person receiving prayer, since this might encourage them to fall. "If it's God," these people argue, "you don't need a catcher."

I agreed for years, not wanting to promote anything fleshly. But this reasoning, when applied to other things of God, is faulty. Try these on for size: "If it's God, you don't need anyone to witness to people. If it's God, you don't need to go to the doctor. If it's God to speak in tongues, you don't need to yield your tongue; the Holy Spirit will do it for you." For the sake of order, and for protection for those who may go down in the flesh, or for those who simply want to yield in order to ensure that they not miss anything the Holy Spirit has for them, it is a good idea to have prayer assistants to stand behind those receiving prayer.

If anyone is afraid to fall and feels impressed to lie down, let the sheep lie down in the pasture. What difference does it make in the eternal scheme? What is the worst that could happen? Someone could make a mistake, fall down, get up and serve Jesus anyway. Believe me, the last time you tripped and fell, you fell for much less.

No one should be made to feel that he must fall or that he is unspiritual if he does not. Do not compare yourself negatively *or* positively with those who fall in response to prayer, and do not prohibit anyone from falling. Give room for the Holy Spirit to do what He wants.

Let God Have Control

Allowing the Holy Spirit to move on people freely is one of the big issues in a day of visitation. Whether or not we understand everything completely, we must allow Jesus headship over His Church. This includes setting aside prejudices and fears and giving Him control and authority. In another chapter we will discuss some of the practical aspects leaders face. For now, let me say simply that physical manifestations produce in a congregation awe at God's ability to change lives and bring forth fruit. When people see that He is able to move in such a way, it gives them hope for deeper change.

God is stirring the Holy Spirit within people who have allowed gifts to lie dormant for years. Many of the manifestations occur as the Holy Spirit makes His first powerful move on individuals. The manifestations may not be a permanent fixture in people's spiritual lives. But we must allow the Spirit to move on His people this way as long as He likes. Believers who submit to the Holy Spirit when He moves in this way are permitting the Lord to bring into their lives the revelation of Himself in this day of visitation that He wants them to have. They will begin to lose their inhibitions and fear of man in many areas, including worship, witnessing, serving and manifesting the gifts of the Holy Spirit.

As time goes on, the manifestations may change. They may deepen in intensity or disappear altogether. Some may remain as keys that open the door to a constant refilling of the Holy Spirit. In any case, the deposit the Holy Spirit leaves of joy at the sense of His presence is worth our accommodating ourselves to this form of change.

One final word. That some individuals have manifestations and then fall away says nothing about the manifestations and a lot about *them*. The power that overcame the guards who arrested Jesus was real, but they did not allow the experience to change their behavior. Judas, too, saw signs and wonders, followed Jesus closely for three years, but did not allow the experience to make lasting changes in his character. This does not mean Jesus is not the Son of God. It means we must allow ourselves not only to be overcome by His power, but to be changed by His love.

Now let's talk about overcoming hindrances to receiving a touch from His hand.

ſ

This Healing River

*N*ick D'Amico is an engineer, a quiet, gentle man married to a vivacious registered nurse. He and Carol have been loved members of our church for nearly ten years and are active in the lives of people in the congregation. Nick and Carol have often drawn themselves out over the less fortunate and have opened their home to the Body of Christ, expecting nothing in return.

The new sense of the Lord's presence had not been visiting us long before Nick and Carol presented themselves at the altar one Sunday for prayer. Carol whispered into my ear some unwelcome news. The doctor had discovered a lump on Nick's body. The doctor, also a Christian, had told him plainly he was concerned and scheduled Nick promptly for a trip to the radiologist at Shadyside Hospital in Pittsburgh.

The D'Amicos' faces offered a somber contrast to the laughter coming from other members at the altar already on the floor under the power of the Spirit.

Their news would elicit a serious, concerned response from other, more sensitive ministers. But suddenly, without warning, a deep laugh rose up inside of me and escaped from my mouth. I heard myself saying, "Well, honey, this is no problem for God!"

Nick and Carol both fell to the carpet and began resting in the Spirit.

As I stepped to the next parishioner waiting for prayer, I thought, *Oh, my, what have I said and done now!* I had no confidence in my ability to pray for the sick. It always seemed that the ones I thought would be healed died, and the scoundrels I thought deserved to die got well! Healing had always been a mystery to me.

The next Sunday, however, Nick was one of the first to testify. He had made his trip to the radiologist. As the technician had scanned the sonogram of his body, he told us, the silence had been deafening.

Oh, no, Nick thought, *it must be serious.*

Then the radiologist came in and looked at the sonogram himself.

"Mr. D'Amico," he said, "why did your doctor send you here? I can't find anything."

The look on Nick's face as he testified in church that Sunday was one of relief and joy. The congregation erupted in laughter, praise and applause, thankful to the Lord Jesus Christ for healing him. The thought that Nick might have contracted a life-threatening illness was something no one had wanted to consider.

Several months later Nick testified again. He thanked God again for his healing, but focused his testimony this time on another aspect of the renewal—the work God had done inside of him. In fact, of the two, Nick prized the internal work of the Spirit as more precious.

Nick D'Amico's healing raised expectations in our church. As the river flowed into the congregation, God renewed our confidence in His healing power. Within a few weeks, we heard four members testify to healings that were confirmed by doctors. Surgeries had been canceled, potentially dangerous health problems removed. The Lord was demonstrating His compassion toward us.

We are not the only ones, of course, experiencing this healing river. Throughout the world, the river is producing similar results.

Streams in Rural England

As the renewal began to flow throughout the world, reports of healings started to circulate. In England, where renewal has been sweeping the land, the river has reached beyond cities into rural settings.

Martin Down is the rector of two neighboring rural Church of England parishes nestled in the countryside of East Anglia in Norfolk,

England. On a sunny Sunday morning, he stands robed in his white cassock, waiting at the door of St. George's, whose church bell tower was built in 1497. The churchyard of St. George's is full of grave markers grown over with deep, green grass, some of them leaning, propped up with stones, many dating back hundreds of years. The church bells peal out over the sleeping village of Saham Toney—the joyful signal that the service is about to begin. Faithful Anglicans begin to make their way, as they have for hundreds of years, into the old flint sanctuary to sit in ornately carved pews older than the United States of America.

But something new is happening at St. George's. When Martin Down and his wife, Maureen, read about the Toronto Blessing, they journeyed to Ontario hungry for more of God and for His presence to flow more powerfully into their parishes. They were not disappointed. The river of blessing has been bringing spiritual refreshing to two parishes.

To the question "How do you know this visitation is of God?" Martin replies without hesitation, "The changed lives." Indeed, the congregations are alive with an air of expectancy and simple faith that have been honored by the Holy Spirit's power.

Jill

Jill Starkey came to Saham Toney from the city more than two years ago. A Christian for about ten years, she prayed a prayer once to be filled with the Holy Spirit, but nothing much happened until she came to Saham Toney. When she arrived she started attending the Alpha course, a ten-week study for inquirers into the Christian faith. God touched her deeply for the first time. Her husband, Ian, noticed that, deep-down, her very character was beginning to change. For years, unable to bear children and having spent much of her life looking after aged parents, she had been full of bitterness. Also, Ian suffered permanent damage from a brain hemorrhage, the result of an accident as a young man; and Jill's resentment, watching his personality change for the worse, only deepened.

But now, as Ian began to notice positive changes in Jill, he decided to attend the Alpha course, too. On the day during the course, when prayers were offered for the Holy Spirit to come and fill everyone in the room, Ian fell on the floor on his hands and knees, laughing deeply for a long time.

During the past twelve months, the damage from the hemorrhage in Ian Starkey's brain has been healed. He is a new person.

The Starkeys are only one family of many who have been touched during this renewal.

Haley

For three years Haley suffered from anorexia nervosa, the emotional illness that affects many high-achieving young women, causing symptoms of depression and the compulsive desire to starve themselves—sometimes to death. By the time Haley arrived at the spring conference in East Anglia sponsored by Living Water, a fellowship of renewed Anglicans, in May 1995, she was sullen and wanted nothing more to do with God. She was tired of getting a little better, then becoming worse and receiving no more than temporary help from stays in the hospital. Still, someone prevailed on her, as she attended the youth event, to get prayer and let God come in and take control.

On the second day of the conference, Haley decided to give the Lord a chance. She came forward for prayer at the end of one of the meetings.

As someone prayed for her, she fell to the floor with the sensation that God was punching her in the stomach. In fact, all night long her body jerked and she grunted, continuing to feel "punches." The following day Haley received more prayer, only to have the manifestation continue.

But the Lord took away the anorexia, filled her with His Spirit and restored her appetite. Since May 1995 Haley has been free of symptoms. The Lord did more for her in a few hours than anyone had been able to do in years of counseling.

Streams of Living Water

These are only two stories of the recent effects of the river of God's blessing flowing through these two churches in the countryside of Norfolk, England. Another woman, incapacitated recently with excruciating back pain for which medication brought no relief, found the pain disappear completely as she received soaking prayer. Prayer enabled her to function again normally.

Both of these Anglican parishes have been affected so powerfully that Martin is writing a book, *Streams of Living Water* (Monarch), about the effects of the current renewal upon them.

Healing Emotions

At Church of the Risen Saviour, the healing power of the Lord Jesus Christ found a new dimension of release within weeks after members began receiving prayer. The furrowed brows and downcast countenances that once stared back at Bill and me as we stood in the pulpit were being changed into mirrors of newfound peace.

The Hot Flash Club

The summer of 1994 was difficult emotionally for several of us women. I had endured a hysterectomy and complications that resulted in infections. Then, as my estrogen level took an unexpected, dramatic drop, I was plunged into hormone shock, which resulted in panic attacks. These exacted a painful toll from my already discouraged emotions. I would wake up at night trembling in terror, as though something awful were about to happen to me. The fear of disease—a fear from which the Lord had freed me twenty years before—began pressing in on me.

I had once been a fun-loving, positive person. Now, shell-shocked by the trauma of surgery and the tragedies that surrounded me in the lives of other church members, I felt the devastation of mental agony. At times I thought I would lose my mind.

But after November, through repeated soaking in prayer, the Lord gradually lifted the darkness, without anti-depressant medications, and replaced it with tranquillity and joy.

Several other women in the congregation had been suffering depression and fear as a result of the natural onset of the change of life. When we discovered we were all suffering similar emotional and physical symptoms, we decided to form a support group and meet for dinner at a nice restaurant once a month, in the hopes that talking about it would help. We informally dubbed ourselves "The Hot Flash Club."

Not long after renewal began, I noticed the entire Hot Flash Club down on the carpet at the altar one night under the influence of the Holy Spirit. Everyone was engaged with the Lord and experiencing waves of peace and joy washing over their previously tormented emotions.

Shirley Nardina, one of the most faithful women in our congregation and a member of the Hot Flash Club, had not smiled much in three years—at least, not with her heart. As the power of the Holy Spirit fell on Shirley, she began to be transformed by laughter. In her mind's eye, as she testified later, she saw heaven open up and caught a glimpse of the atmosphere there. Heaven, she saw, was in a constant state of rejoicing. Suddenly aware of the victory we have in Christ, she felt like shouting praises to Jesus. But out of her mouth came the words "Hip, hip, hooray! Three cheers for Jesus!"—for more than two hours. She felt a renewed sense of the love of God for her. As she lay on the floor laughing and praising Him, she realized that some parishioners on the floor around her were also exulting in the Lord. She sensed everyone being uplifted by the love of God from trying circumstances.

Several months later, Shirley's husband, Ron, had to give up his job because of heart problems. For several days Shirley felt anxiety about the future beginning to press in on her. One night she awoke with the strongest anxiety attack she had had—much stronger than the ones she had experienced before the renewal. Despite much prayer and a sense of victory, now she felt swallowed up, overwhelmed by spiritual battle.

Then into her left ear she heard a song, a new melody she had never heard before, and the words *God will take care of you*. For two hours it seemed that an angel was singing to her, soothing her and lifting her spirit to enable her to be victorious in the spiritual fight.

Two weeks later Bill mentioned in a sermon that he had been praying over every person at the altar, "Lord, give them songs in the night." Shirley was startled and realized that her pastor's prayers for her had been answered. Peace returned.

In church on December 17, 1995, just a week before Christmas, Shirley's husband presented the pastors' Christmas gifts from the congregation. Ron had built a model of a church building, covered it with silver wrapping paper and fixed it so the roof could be removed. He talked about the peace God had given him during the renewal, recounted the joys and sorrows the congregation had faced this year and thanked the pastors on behalf of everyone for their labors of love. Then he sat down next to Shirley.

As Bill opened the Bible and began his message, suddenly Ron slumped over onto his wife. Without a sign of pain, he went to be with the Lord.

Since Ron's death, Shirley has grieved through periods of extreme sadness. The thought that her beloved husband of 29 years is gone has been almost impossible to bear. But as she has shared her emotional pain with me, Shirley says that "each day, as my missing Ron grows stronger and stronger, my love for God and His people, and my desire to serve Him, are growing greater at the same time. I have no doubt that, had Ron passed away prior to the renewal, I may have become bitter at God and could not have had the strength to go through this."

Although she shared it with no one at the time, Shirley was aware that whenever the Lord filled her mouth with laughter, it was strengthening her for what was to come. Though she did not want to admit it, deep inside she knew God was going to take Ron home.

"What if I had not responded to the renewal?" Shirley remarked to me recently. "What if I had not been willing to receive prayer? I don't know how I would have lived through this, had it not been for the strength God has given me in this season of renewal."

Repeated fillings of the Holy Spirit have brought Shirley comfort in her grief—and have revived the dashed hopes of the other women as well. They hold a newfound confidence in the power of God to bless their futures and work all things together for their good.

Once They Were Blind, Now They See

One Sunday morning during congregational worship, Jim Arth, retired recently from his job, began to weep loudly as everyone else was singing. This was unlike affable Jim, who often teased the people he loved; no one thought he had a care in the world. The following Sunday Jim testified that the presence of the Lord had surrounded him during worship and lifted a depression he had concealed from everyone. It has not returned.

Older adults are not the only ones being affected by the Lord's loving touch.

Missy Antolec is twenty, a college student who has grown up in our congregation since her mother came to Christ more than twelve years ago. Missy's parents have been divorced all this time. Living without her dad around the house and not being able to experience fatherly affection, Missy paid a heavy price emotionally. She often experienced depression, suffered from low self-esteem and felt like an outsider. At times she even felt suicidal.

But for more than a year, Missy has been soaking in the presence of the Lord, receiving prayer at every service. We often see her on the carpet during the ministry time, smiling peacefully or filled with laughter. As her inner healing began, she began to "see" herself on the lap of her heavenly Father, surrounded by His arms of love and watching a sunset.

At first, she says, she could not believe that her heavenly Father was taking time just to be with her. Once she remarked to Him how beautiful the sunset was. The Lord responded, *Everything I make is beautiful, including you. You're My precious child and I love you.*

As God has begun to restore her wounded soul, Missy's blue eyes shine, her self-confidence restored. As her healing progressed, she began to bring her flute to church and play for her heavenly Father. During the altar service when people are being prayed for, the sound of Missy's flute has soothed people's hearts. Before, she was too shy to try to play in front of others; now she plays solos and spontaneous melodies like a shepherd in a field playing for the sheep.

While Missy understood what the Lord was doing with her, many others have not. All they know is, once they were blind, now they see (see John 9:25).

Linda Pacifico is a women's leader in a church in Bethlehem, Pennsylvania. Since she was a child, she habitually bit her fingernails. Sometimes her fingers were sore and painful, her nails bitten almost to the quick.

When Linda accompanied her pastor's wife, Tricia Groblewski, to services in Toronto, she wanted to receive prayer to take in whatever God had for her. As a member of the prayer team prayed for her, she dropped to the floor, her arms began to flail about and her head began to shake. Her body bounced on the floor so violently that she testified later to carpet burns on her elbows! Yet she sensed God's presence, without understanding what specifically He had done for her. She felt that something had been removed, as if she had had laser surgery.

Two weeks later, shampooing her hair in the shower, she felt her head being scratched gently. She looked down at her fingertips to see that her nails had grown out full-length past the ends of her fingers for the first time in her life!

At the fall women's retreat, Linda dangled her manicured nails over the pulpit as she testified to the inner healing the Lord had given her. She still does not know what He touched; she simply knows that He did. The inner anxiety that caused the nervous habit of nail-biting was gone.

Irene Bell, wife of one of Britain's renewal leaders, Stuart Bell, has always been reticent to speak in public places. Standing before any group, even in her own church, paralyzed her with fear. Whenever the possibility existed that someone might call her to the front, Irene spent anxious hours worrying about it, fearing what might happen if she opened her mouth and nothing came out, or if she said something wrong. If there was the slightest possibility she might be called on, even to say grace before a meal, sometimes she excused herself.

But something happened to Irene through months of receiving prayer and being filled with the Holy Spirit. Not long ago as she and Stuart were gathered for a meal with some of Britain's leaders and their wives, Gerald Coates asked Irene to say grace. Rather than being overtaken by the usual panic, she said to herself, *Well, why not?* She opened her mouth and, to her husband's surprise, prayed aloud in front of everyone. She has since testified before her own church of her healing.

In Acts 4 the entire church prayed for boldness.

> And when they had prayed, the place where they were assembled together was shaken; and they were all filled with the Holy Spirit, and they spoke the word of God with boldness.
>
> Acts 4:31, NKJV

He Restores My Soul

Because Jesus Christ is the Good Shepherd David prophesied about in Psalm 23, any move of the Holy Spirit will accomplish, with God's power, the tasks of a faithful caretaker of the flock. If the current move is really a prelude to widespread revival, it is for the good of the Church. He is leading His flock gently to quiet waters and green pastures where they can be cleansed, watered and fed. The Lord is more grieved than we are, I believe, over the devastation that many of His sheep are experiencing. So the overwhelming sight of these sheep lying in large groups in His presence is enough to revive the hope of any pastor of His flock.

One of my principal concerns for several years has been the emotional state of God's people. How can a child of the Master, limping through life with unhealed emotional wounds, or devastated by grief over disappointed hopes, help to gather in a harvest of souls in a time of revival? Today many suffering sheep bear witness that a dimension of the Holy Spirit's power to bind up the brokenhearted has been missing in the Church.

At a conference in Toronto in October 1995, as I lay on the floor, I felt an unusual sense of the Lord's soothing presence. I "saw" myself coming upon a wounded man lying by the road in the middle of a wilderness. Feeling compassion for him, I began scanning the surroundings looking for raw materials to bind up his wounds. I found a crudely shaped stick and bound his arm with a scrap of cloth torn from something I had with me. I sat beside the man, my eyes scanning the horizon anxiously, waiting for help to arrive.

Even as I lay on the floor, the Holy Spirit gave me the interpretation:

There are many like you who couldn't pass the wounded by. You are like the good Samaritan, who did the best he could with what he had. But a day is coming when what you have been able to do for people now will seem like applying first aid. You will see help from the throne of God, a powerful anointing of the Lord to do what you have to this moment only wished you could.

In that moment I experienced a release of guilt that had been projected onto me by criticism and misunderstanding from others. I realized I had not grieved the Lord, but that He knew I knew I had confidence in Him. The only thing I did not know was how long it would take Him to arrive.

I believe we are going to see more release of the healing power of the Lord as revival comes. Are these healings significant? Ask those who are being healed. Do they attribute the healings to Jesus Christ? What does the presence of healing mean? Nothing—unless the healings glorify God the Father and the Lord Jesus Christ. This is how we know the Holy Spirit is at work.

Some say we should not trust that form of evidence—implying that unless something is totally traditional and appears letter for letter in Scripture, it could not possibly produce anything godly. But this is the attitude the Pharisees had when Jesus healed people on the Sabbath. Disregarding the display of His awesome power, they quibbled over whether it was scriptural. When the man lame for 38 years picked up his bed and walked away from the portico of the pool of Bethesda, the Pharisees wanted to know if this was a scriptural manifestation. But the Lord Himself told us to believe Him for His works' sake:

> "If I do not do the works of My Father, do not believe Me; but if I do them, though you do not believe Me, believe the works, that you may know and understand that the Father is in Me, and I in the Father."
>
> John 10:37–38

If the miracles of inner healing we are now seeing take place on a widespread scale are a harbinger of things to come, we need to prepare ourselves to see God's power make our crude methods obsolete. I wonder how we will react if the day comes when God's children do not need our help anymore! I think I will be glad.

But not only does the Lord heal to relieve the sufferings of His children. In addition, manifestations of the healing power of God draw attention to the fact that He is moving, as happened in Debra Petrosky's life.

The Children's Bread

An hour before the first service of our renewal weekend in August 1995, Debra Petrosky arrived early to make sure she got a seat.

An articulate professional woman, freelance writer and editor, Debra serves on the worship team of her church. Three years before, on a day she had set aside for prayer and fasting, a car accident disrupted her life. A teenager with a new license cut across her path as she drove through a green light. Both vehicles were totaled.

After the accident she saw an orthopedic doctor, a physical therapist and a chiropractor for her injuries. Accustomed to an active life, Debra was dismayed to discover that just a few minutes of walking now caused debilitating headaches. Sometimes she took ten to twelve Tylenol a day, and needed to lie down frequently to take pressure off her neck. This put a crunch in the home-based business she had just started, and her income plummeted. The chronic pain and loss of income contributed to depression.

The Holy Spirit touched Debra's life dramatically in June 1995 when she visited Hosanna Church in Pittsburgh. Gary and Donna Paladin, the pastor and his wife, had returned recently from Toronto.

During the ministry time at Hosanna Church, Debra fell under the power of the Spirit and found her long-standing depression lifted.

Then came our August renewal weekend. At the conclusion of the Friday evening service, we stacked the chairs and asked those who wanted prayer to stand for ministry. As a member of the ministry team laid hands on Debra, she fell to the carpet and found her arms moving back and forth. Her sense of God's power increased; then her head began to shake vigorously from side to side.

Lord, I hope this is my healing, she prayed. *If it's not, I'm going to be really sore tomorrow!*

Her physical manifestations lasted nearly an hour. Checking her neck, Debra noticed that the muscles were unusually supple.

At home after the meeting, she noticed an odd-shaped crust of bread a few inches below her pillow. She had not eaten in her bedroom and did not know where it had come from. As she popped the morsel into her mouth, a Scripture passage dropped into her mind, one she had read in her devotional time that very morning—the passage in which the Canaanite woman begged Jesus to heal her daughter (see Matthew 15:22–28). Jesus had told the woman, "It is not good to take the children's bread and throw it to the dogs" (verse 26). The woman replied, "Yes, Lord; but even the dogs feed on the crumbs which fall from their masters' table" (verse 27). Debra began to wonder if she, too, had begun to taste the divine crumbs.

The next morning, Saturday, she went to the track to walk. As she finished her fourth lap—her limit since the accident—she felt the Lord say, *Take a victory lap!* She began to run. Checking her neck over the next half-mile, she began to say aloud, "I've got the children's bread! I'm healed!" She traveled another mile—running, walking and rejoicing all the way. As hour after hour passed with no stiffness and no headache, she realized she had been miraculously healed.

On Sunday the power of the Holy Spirit descended on Debra again in her own church. As the worship team prayed before the service, she became "drunk" in the Spirit and fell to the floor. The other pastors, standing in for the pastor on vacation, did not know what to think. But knowing Debra to be stable and mature, they "handled" the scene as best they could.

But it was too late. The curiosity of all who knew her was irreversibly pricked, and the Holy Spirit kindled renewal fire in her local church.

Renewal of Gifts of Healing

Nancy Westerberg, the quiet, reserved children's pastor who asked me to dance with her in church, made a scheduled trip to the gynecologist a few days after the Holy Spirit fell on her. One cyst in her breast, which had been monitored for four years, had already been removed surgically. Now she learned that another one, which had been monitored for two years, had suddenly disappeared.

Encouraged to see the power of God move in her own body, Nancy began to lay hands on her husband each night as he slept. Bert had been scheduled for the surgical removal of a large cyst on his leg, which had caused him to limp for more than a year. Nothing had helped; surgery was thought the only solution. But every night Nancy prayed simply, "More of You, Jesus. More of Your Spirit." As she prayed, the cyst gradually disappeared and Bert's surgery was canceled.

Ruth Madeira, a breakfast waitress at a local coffee shop, heard about the moving of the Holy Spirit from Bill and me as she waited on our table. Ruth began to visit our church and receive prayer. Joy returned to her life. Then, a few weeks later, she failed a stress test during her yearly physical. The doctor feared her arteries were blocked. But as Ruth continued to soak in prayer at the altar, the Lord gave her an overwhelming sense of peace. We were thrilled when her angiogram showed she did not need surgery. Ruth now serves on the ministry team praying for others.

As a new surge of healing power flows through the Church, the Body of Christ is beginning to pray for the sick more often, simply asking the Holy Spirit to come and touch as He chooses.

Recently a young teenager, Tiffany Sines, who participates in our puppet ministry serving nursing homes, fell on the steps at church. Her ankle begin to swell immediately. Carol, our "resident R.N.," feared a torn ligament. Members of the church, including kids playing nearby, gathered around her for prayer. Then her mother put her into the car and headed for the emergency room.

As they approached the hospital, Tiffany looked at her ankle and asked her mother to pull over by the side of the road. The swelling had gone down completely. Bouncing up and down in excitement, Tiffany put her shoe on, went back to church and helped with the puppet ministry that very afternoon. Carol, the nurse, told me later she knew Tiffany's ankle had been seriously injured and that there was no way it could have repaired itself in that short a time.

Before renewal broke out in our church, praying for the sick had become perfunctory, something we did because we knew it was right. Many we had prayed for seemed to experience nothing. Every so often someone would improve, but we could not tell if it was the natural healing process or the miraculous power of the Holy Spirit. Even natural healing is a gift from God, but when people became seriously ill, we had little faith to pray for them.

Not all have been healed who have suffered physical problems since the renewal began. But even those who have not have found renewed strength to stand and face the trial with a sense of God's tender, watchful care rather than feeling abandoned in their hour of need.

When I pray, "More, Lord!" in this renewal, one of my desires is for more demonstrations of His healing power.

How Can I Experience His Healing?

The healing power of God that we have been experiencing has come in direct response to the cries of His children for more of their heavenly Father's presence in their lives. The healings have come by His sovereignty as He is given the opportunity to touch each one and bring whatever manifestation He chooses.

At the same time, there is much scriptural evidence for beseeching the Lord specifically to heal. If healing is an important concern for you, continue to receive prayer as often as possible and respond to the inner promptings of the Holy Spirit. But continue to set aside your own agenda. You may not remember that your heavenly Father knows what you have need of before the request leaves your lips (see Matthew 6:8). So keep asking for more of Him, and do not be surprised when you sense His healing power flowing through you; or when you discover, without feeling anything at all, that your ailment or disease is gone.

Pray for others to be healed, too, asking the Lord especially to come on them in the way He desires.

During seasons of refreshing and revival, the Lord visits His people with signs and wonders for the purpose of restoring their awe in the demonstrations of His merciful power. All He needs is room to move. Give Him every opportunity to do so.

Now let's look at how a local church can open its doors to the blessing and cooperate with the Lord to fan the flames of the refreshing—and perhaps see full-scale revival.

6

Preparing for the Blessing

Receiving the blessings of renewal is like jumping into a river and allowing yourself to be carried along. But what if you are afraid of the water? Paul Blackham, the worship leader I mentioned in chapter 4 (who, with his wife, Jennie, returned to our church), testified before the congregation after being touched by the Lord, "I wasn't afraid that it wasn't God; I was afraid that it was, and that I would have to face Him."

The fear of facing God and of perhaps being passed over by Him haunts many of God's children. A visitation from the Lord is a precious time, a time when He seems to bend down and kiss the earth, drawing near to His children and to the lost world. But it is estimated that nearly one quarter of those in every congregation fear they will find themselves remaining in their seats, or even standing for prayer, receiving nothing while everyone else gets blessed. Many of us tend to believe God will pass us by.

Sometimes the excuses we make—especially our theological ones—are just covers for fear. Maybe you have trouble admitting *you* are afraid. But preparing your heart to receive the blessings of renewal necessitates taking a look at the reasons you may be afraid.

Before the flood, Noah had to spend time building the ark. Before the Lord came in glory to Israel, they had to build the Tabernacle. God told Elisha that Jehoshaphat was to make the valley full of ditches. Elisha told the widow without food or resources to borrow vessels from her neighbor: "Do not get a few" (2 Kings 4:3). He promised that her jar of oil would be multiplied to fill every vessel.

The point is, before God moves, He asks us to prepare.

Prepare to Contain the Blessing

Some years ago the Lord impressed our church that we should prepare to contain the blessing. We even made a banner and hung it on
the wall behind the pulpit to remind us to ready ourselves for what
God would do. But it is difficult to prepare for something unseen and
unknown. All we could do was surrender to the Holy Spirit's leading
day after day (some days more successfully than others).

Then, in 1986, Bill and I found ourselves in the middle of the Christian recovery movement, which was addressing the emotional pain
of those brought up in homes with alcoholism and abuse. We were
shocked to discover that ninety percent of the members of our own
church fell into this category! Most of our brothers and sisters were
suffering and we had not even realized it. Many lived without being
able to experience love. Still others suffered secretly from addictions
they felt were too shameful to disclose in a Christian setting.

As Bill and I began to study to gain practical knowledge about the
human soul, we began to see how our own lives had been affected by
our experiences. Although our families were different from theirs, we
shared many of the same emotional inhibitions. I have written exten-
sively about these issues in my other books. But I did not realize until
recently that my healing process was part of a chain of preparatory events
leading to my reception of what God would do next. The knowledge I
was gaining about my emotional weaknesses would help me learn not
to quench the Holy Spirit, but rather to fan His flame in my soul.

"Let Me Love You"

In chapter 2 we observed that we can miss a move of the Holy Spirit
when we cherish preconceived notions of what a revival should be like.

John Arnott, pastor of the Toronto Fellowship, was disturbed early
in the outpouring because his own idea of revival included numerous new commitments to Christ. He began to try to direct the flow
toward the lost. When he did, however, he sensed a struggle, as if he

was resisting the Holy Spirit. When he prayed about it, the Lord spoke in terms John could understand: *Is it all right with you if I love up on My Church for a while?*

We who tend to place a higher value on results than God does (like the Ephesian church in the book of Revelation) will see little value in the current blessing. In this framework, every move of God is measured by the number of grains of wheat in the harvest.

What is happening now, by contrast, is the Holy Spirit's work to renew in Jesus' bride a deep love for Him that will become the underlying motivation for all future work. Bill believes that out of this move of God will come an army of missionaries to gather in the waiting harvest out of love for Him. Enjoying what God is doing now depends on your being able to open the shut-off valve of your spiritual heart and let Him love you. We cannot be fruitful without receiving love.

Revival, according to Jonathan Edwards, is manifested on two fronts: the salvation of sinners and the quickening of the saints. What we are seeing now is a quickening of our love for Jesus that makes our countenances glow and the world take notice. Fresh oil is being poured into empty lampstands.

But what if there are subconscious hindrances to our being able to receive love? What prevents us from being able to receive?

Letting God Touch Us

The apostle Peter, one of Jesus' closest friends and disciples, found it difficult at first to receive from Jesus. He was happy to have been chosen to follow Him, but was certain up to Jesus' crucifixion that his selection was based on the fact that the Lord needed him. Peter refused to believe he was capable of denying Jesus, and in the Garden of Gethsemane pulled out his sword to provide Jesus with security services.

Everyone is amused at times by the blustering, ingenuous sayings and deeds of Peter. We all know people like him who express every observation that comes to mind and have the entire Christian walk analyzed and condensed into pithy quips. We may not recognize, however, that we ourselves are like Peter in our unwillingness to present ourselves for ministry. Receiving from the Lord is harder for us than serving Him.

During the Last Supper, Jesus performed a humbling act of affection and service for His most trusted friends. After dinner He laid aside His cloak, placed a towel around His waist and began to wash the feet of each disciple. They had walked with Him faithfully for three years and given up everything to follow Him. Now, as He offered an act of love and model for their future treatment of one another, everyone cooperated—except Peter. When Jesus reached him, he withdrew his feet. He did not believe he needed this experience. He could wash his own feet. After all, he was one of the closest disciples and devoted to his Master. What Jesus was doing made no sense.

But Jesus shocked him with His insistence. "What I do you do not realize now, but you shall understand hereafter" (John 13:7). It is not necessary, in other words, to understand what God is doing. All we need to know is that Jesus wants to touch us.

But Jesus went further. "If I do not wash you, you have no part with Me" (verse 8). *No* in the Greek means "no."

Jesus was doing something new to each of His disciples, something He had never done before. It may have been embarrassing and uncomfortable emotionally. Obviously they did not understand it. But unless they allowed Him to do what He wanted to, they could have no part of ministry with Him.

Giving out in ministry is directly proportional to our willingness and ability to receive from Jesus. It does not matter if you are one of His closest disciples or have a dynamic and powerful ministry or hold a position of authority in the Body of Christ; if the Lord Jesus tells you to reach out your foot, it is time to do it! Regardless of our realm of responsibility or place of dignity, we desperately need His touch.

Surely the word *dignity* is epitomized in David Edwards, president emeritus of Elim Bible Institute in Lima, New York. He holds a prominent place among charismatic and Pentecostal leaders and is an elder of Elim Fellowship, one of the oldest and most respected Pentecostal streams in the world, overseeing churches and pastors in many countries. David articulates profound insight with a Welsh accent, and his gracious demeanor, tall stature and silver-white hair and beard create an imposing presence.

His first contact with the renewal came through the ministry of Rodney Howard-Browne at Carpenter's Home Church in Lakeland, Florida. "The longer I watched him," recounts David Edwards, "the more convinced I became of his integrity." As David and his wife, Mefus, drove to Elim the following week for their annual conference, he stopped in North Carolina and happened to purchase Jack Hayford's book *Desire for Fullness*.

"I was quite convicted by what he had to say," David continues. "I had to ask myself whether I was as eager and strenuous in my pursuit of all that God had for me as I had been before I retired. I recognized this as another wave of renewal that God was sending His Church. I prayed and said, *Lord, I don't want to be on the sidelines. I don't want to be a spectator. I certainly don't want to be a critic.* It is often said that those most likely to be hostile toward a renewal are those who were last affected by a visitation from God. I certainly didn't want that to happen to me."

Of the fifteen meetings at Elim that week, David was able to attend thirteen. He stood for prayer at every one, but did not seem to receive the blessing he sought.

"Eventually," he explains, "more by accident than anything, I was accosted by a 'catcher' who said, 'Would you like to be prayed for?' I didn't have the courage to say no."

It was then that the power of God began to touch David Edwards. He fell to the floor under the power of the Holy Spirit.

He did not realize that some members of Elim Fellowship were watching him. One of them remarked in his daughter's presence, "I'll know this visitation is of God if David Edwards goes down!" Another of his former students remarked, "If David Edwards goes down, the next event will be the Rapture!"

"Although the Rapture has not yet happened," David says with a twinkle, "both of those who watched me are now convinced this visitation is real."

The reaction of a man like David Edwards to the current wave of renewal demonstrates how we should respond to Jesus' desire to touch our lives in a new way: with keen discernment, earnest longing, continual searching and humble yieldedness. If what we see moving through the Church today is truly a work of the Spirit, we must acknowledge it and honor the desire of the Lord Jesus to touch us personally with His Holy Spirit. If Jesus is showing up in the Church to touch His bride with an outpouring of His Spirit, we must find a way to allow Him the utmost liberty to do so.

Jonathan Edwards in "Distinguishing Marks of the Work of the Spirit of God" said it this way: "Now Christ is come down from heaven in a remarkable and wonderful work of his Spirit, it becomes all his professed disciples to acknowledge him, and give him honour" (*Edwards on Revival*, p. 130).

Why Is Receiving Difficult?

What are some of the hindrances to our being able to receive the love and blessings of God?

"I Don't Understand It"

Perhaps Peter's reason for withdrawing his feet from the hands of Jesus is the same reason you have difficulty: You do not understand what He is doing. Some people feel they must understand and analyze everything before they embrace or surrender to it.

This is funny, when you think about it. We cannot grasp the mysteries of God—mysteries like salvation, the Trinity, His love for us sinners and many others. We accept them by faith. If we lived to be a thousand, we would not comprehend a thimbleful of God in comparison to what He knows!

Even so, each child of God receives the new birth before he or she understands much of it; and it is necessary to become childlike in order to receive anything from God. "Unless you are converted and become like children," said Jesus, "you shall not enter the kingdom of heaven" (Matthew 18:3). Children do not need to understand and analyze in order to appreciate. They simply relish the moment. In fact, the mystery of things is part of the wonder of the moment for them.

Jesus explained patiently to Peter at the Last Supper what we *all* need to hear. We may not understand what He wants to do for each of us in this renewal, as we receive prayer and a touch from His Spirit, but we must open our hearts to Him nevertheless and let Him do what He wants.

Drs. Lowell and Marie Hoffman, the clinical psychologists I mentioned in chapter 4, have observed people on the carpet under the power of the Holy Spirit, being healed of traumas without even understanding what was taking place. Some people, the Hoffmans explain, bury painful traumas so deep that they are impossible to recall. Recollecting them, in fact, would mean reliving the events and experiencing even more devastating pain. (In false memory syndrome, by contrast, people seem to recall painful experiences that never occurred. The mind has mistakenly embedded fleeting thoughts as memories.) During the present renewal, the Hoffmans have found the Holy Spirit healing tormenting memories without the pain of recall. Unaware of what God was doing, men and women have experienced His healing power anyway.

Other people are aware of what God is healing.

Shirley Nardina, whom we met in chapter 5, grew up in a home where her father was a binge drinker. Sober, he was a strong disciplinarian, controlling and mean. Drunk, he shouted and placed the whole family in fear of his anger. By the time he died, Shirley had never known warmth or love from him. Many hurts she buried and refused to remember. Some lay so deep she could not remember them, even if she had wanted to.

One Sunday night John Carr, a visiting minister from Dundee, Scotland, was speaking about his realization that he was the "Father's little child." Suddenly the Lord spoke to Shirley: *You haven't known Me as Father.* At that moment she realized she had always prayed to Jesus and had always wanted to be a friend to the Holy Spirit, but had subconsciously resisted relating to the Lord as Father.

She went forward and fell at the altar. As sobs rolled over her, she felt that she was "travailing"—as though she were giving birth, but spiritually rather than physically. Years of anger, hurt and pain were released in a wave of forgiveness toward the father she had hated. In their place, peace about him began to cover her. And a block was removed between Shirley and her heavenly Father.

She told me recently she had never realized how much the Father loved her until this renewal. It is in part a renewal of the Father's love.

We must be willing to give to the Lord our right to understand everything before we open up to Him. All we need to know is that it is Jesus who wants to touch us—which brings up another difficulty: the fear of receiving a false experience or even a false spirit.

Fear of Receiving a False Spirit

The fear of being deceived by a false spirit is a major hindrance to many earnest Christians. Paul warned that in the last days "some will fall away from the faith, paying attention to deceitful spirits and doctrines of demons" (1 Timothy 4:1). Every spirit yields some kind of fruit, but the fruit of a wrong spirit is as obvious as the fruit of the Holy Spirit. It isolates and leads into sin, thereby subtracting glory from Jesus Christ. The key words here are *fall away from the faith.* Such people always fall away from the Body of Christ, isolating themselves from correction and the protection of the Church.

Let's note that Paul was *not* writing this warning to the earnest Christian seeking a more intimate relationship with Jesus Christ.

The fear of being seduced by a false spirit came up often during the decades of charismatic renewal regarding the issue of speaking in tongues. Some people were afraid their gifts would not be genuine, that a false spirit would prompt them if they attempted to yield their tongues to the Lord and speak out.

Nothing could be further from the truth. I have been privileged to pray for many who sought to be baptized in the Holy Spirit, and never once have I encountered any earnest seeker who received a false spirit or a false tongue. I have never heard of it from anyone else in the Pentecostal or charismatic sectors of the Body of Christ either.

Fear of Getting into the Flesh

Still another reason for reluctance to yield to renewal is the fear of being deceived by one's own enthusiasm. Some believers are afraid that, rather than receive from the Holy Spirit, they will instead fall into the flesh. I appreciate this concern but have to admit it amuses me. We should be as cautious about entering into sin! When the opportunity to gossip presents itself, I never hear anyone ask, "Do you think I might be getting into the flesh?" Times like those are when we should fear the flesh most!

Internationally known Bible teacher Iverna Tompkins encouraged the pastors at a conference recently not to fear that flesh might get into the renewal. "The flesh isn't scary," she said. "It's just boring!"

The truth is, we spend the better part of each day in the flesh, and will until the day we die or Jesus comes back. All of us are flesh and spirit. In the new covenant, the treasure of the Spirit is always found in an earthen vessel. The Holy Spirit within has chosen to seep out to others through us. The impact of the power of God's Spirit touching us can be so strong that our natural faculties react and even become disoriented.

Jack Groblewski, pastor of New Covenant Christian Community Church in Bethlehem, Pennsylvania, likens people's responses to the Holy Spirit in this renewal to sticking one's finger in an electric socket without a light bulb in place. It would be odd indeed if the presence of God invaded us and nothing out of the ordinary happened! Since the flesh profits nothing one way or the other, it is far better to risk yielding to impressions and impulses that are likely to be the Holy Spirit, and coming up with nothing, than to miss the reality of His presence because we are afraid of getting into the flesh.

It is necessary in these days, I believe, for pastors to afford greater latitude for emotional expression in order to accommodate renewal in our churches. Bill and I have decided it is far better to see a few emotional excesses than to make the mistake of cutting off the Holy Spirit's work in someone's life.

Jesus encouraged us to press on to receive all our heavenly Father has to offer. There is always more to Him than we have experienced. So Jesus urged us to "ask, and it will be given to you; seek, and you will find; knock, and it will be opened to you" (Luke 11:9, NKJV). But along with that, He promised to guard our prayers, and the answers to those prayers, with His protection:

> "If a son asks for bread from any father among you, will he give him a stone? Or if he asks for a fish, will he give him a serpent instead of a fish? Or if he asks for an egg, will he offer him a scorpion? If you then, being evil, know how to give good gifts to your children, how much more will your heavenly Father give the Holy Spirit to those who ask Him!"
>
> verses 11–13, NKJV

Jesus is saying that our heavenly Father does not tease us, failing to fulfill a request by giving us something painful in response. But those who have been tormented this way throughout their lives by mean authority figures may find this promise difficult to believe. Many testify to a release into an ability to trust God when they asked the Lord to help them forgive their abusers. Some may need special counseling and further assurance before they are ready to trust. But continuing to seek means we will eventually be able to open the shut-off valve and receive a filling of His love.

Another group with difficulty receiving are those who cannot be convinced that the Scriptures support the experiences of those who claim to have received God's blessing. In chapter 4 we looked at some of the scriptural support for the uncommon manifestations many seem to be experiencing.

Not only do some people fear getting in the flesh themselves, but they seem to be put off from receiving if they are afraid others around them are manifesting fleshly responses. How many people received healings and blessings from Jesus as they pressed through crowds of people who were full of every kind of evil motive? Even if you suspect that some people receiving prayer in your vicinity are "in the flesh," it does not mean you will be, too. In fact, you need only seek Jesus yourself for more of His love and the fullness of His Spirit in your life. Touch Him by faith and leave others around you to God. They cannot stop you from receiving unless you allow what they are doing to offend you. So tune them out.

Fear of Emotional Reactions

The fear of emotional reactions is another difficulty that prevents some sincere Christians from receiving a touch from God. They are convinced the Lord will "explode" within them and cause them to behave in a manner contrary to their best judgment. So you hear this verse quoted: "Let all things be done decently and in order" (1 Corinthians 14:40, KJV). The apostle Paul, however (contrary to the assumptions of these Bible-quoting Christians), believed in allowing the Holy Spirit to reign in the Church.

When we feel uncomfortable with someone's emotional intensity, we tend to use our feelings as the thermometer for judging the validity of their experience. Numerous times in this renewal, my own comfort zone has been invaded by people who got "too emotional." But the Scriptures are full of people who carried on in the presence of Jesus Christ. Some responded emotionally with shouting or crying out for mercy. Others invaded parties or went to great lengths to get His attention. Jesus rebuked demons, but in no case did He rebuke a single person for an emotional outburst. (Rather, it is the servant devoid of the emotion of love whom Jesus rebuked in Revelation 2:4–5.)

Our emotions were given to us by God to enable us to enjoy His fullness and find release from the tension that comes when we feel very deeply. The more vulnerable we are, the more open we will be emotionally. Humility and vulnerability go together. It makes no sense to purport that the fullness of the Holy Spirit—which Paul equates with deep joy, drunkenness, groanings too deep for words and the unfathomable riches of Christ—can be experienced without emotion. Living in the Spirit *does* involve the emotions (as well as the mind and will), and is designed to make an impact that will last forever.

Fear of Abandonment

Some are hindered by fear they will be left out of what God is doing. Paul Blackham articulated this fear at the beginning of the chapter. These people are braced already for the moment when this renewal will end and they are left in the same state as before. Perhaps such folks were abandoned as children (or even as adults) and find it difficult to believe the Lord will truly never leave them nor forsake them.

Some who have faced severe trials, such as divorce or the loss of a loved one, may have particular difficulty. It is as though the ground has split open beneath them and they cannot trust it again.

My friend Beverly, who has observed me trying to receive over and over, perceived that I was afraid the Lord would take off again and leave me behind. Sometimes as I begin to receive a touch from the Lord, I feel like shutting myself off or that I am losing focus. The more often I receive prayer, the more this tendency has diminished. But if you want to pray for me, pray for that!

Fear of Losing Control

The group with the greatest difficulty receiving is the one that stands as sentinels in the Church: the Lord's ministers.

One of the curious things I noticed about the services in Toronto was the large number of pastors from all over the globe. It is difficult for a pastor to be touched in his or her own church. The responsibility of making sure everyone else is receiving, and the habit of being selfless in every service, inhibit pastors' opportunities to receive. Then there are the expectations of others quick to criticize if the pastor fails them or if he is seen in an undignified pose. And finally, pastors are generally possessed with a need to control. (I speak from personal experience.)

Other members of the Body of Christ who have grown up in homes where violence, abuse or lack of nurturing made them feel insecure are also preoccupied (subconsciously or otherwise) with the need to control their environments. They are used to managing situations and organizing everyone into disciplined regiments. Some people are natural-born managers who believe they are gifted by God to administer every arena in which they find themselves. More than once, since my own responsibility on the pastoral staff of our church has been to administer, I have become preoccupied with organizing renewal meetings and have heard the Lord say, *Let Me love you.*

Relinquishing control of a situation in which ministry is occurring, and then actually receiving a blessing yourself, is foreign to many ministers who receive only two weeks of vacation a year, much less opportunities to travel to receive ministry themselves. Even on retreats they are generally in a learning mode, looking for ways to make the church grow or for new recipes for serving the Scriptures to hungry sheep. Men in particular feel more comfortable in spiritual situations in which they are required to perform.

But this renewal is not about doing or about acquiring knowledge. It is about opening our spirits to the powerful touch of His love.

Men need love, too, but the idea of being swept off your feet by Jesus Christ is difficult for many of them to accept. Some even have to force themselves to be romantic with their own wives. No wonder "Coach" is such a popular show on TV! Craig T. Nelson portrays a football coach accustomed to facing every situation with testosterone-empowered solutions. But when it comes to his wife, Christine, he is a pussycat. He has to force himself to learn to talk about feelings and be a "sensitive man of the '90s."

But the emotional relationship between husband and wife foreshadows the powerful love relationship between Jesus Christ and His bride. This is not something perverse but pure and holy. Men as well as women need permission to surrender their feelings to the Lord without fear of improper love or even lust.

During this renewal many men have testified to the powerful emotional experience of being overshadowed by the love of Jesus and of having returned to their first love. The apostle John characterized himself as "the disciple whom Jesus loved" (John 21:20) because he had come to know the love of Jesus.

One of the most touching testimonies I have heard from the platform in Toronto, in my numerous visits, was from an evangelist from Finland. His wife had suffered terribly during a nine-year battle with brain cancer. During the four years since her death, he had gone everywhere to try to regain his feelings for life and for the Lord. Everyone he knew had prayed for him. His last resort had been to come to Toronto to see if God would meet him. That afternoon he had attended the meeting in which the ministry team prays only for full-time pastors and their spouses. For more than four hours this evangelist had lain on the floor as waves of Jesus' love had swept over him. By the time the renewal meeting began that evening, he had to be helped to the platform by two men, one under each arm. He could scarcely talk, so caught up was he in the love of Jesus.

As he testified, tears streamed down my face. Love for my Lord is, above all things, what I want from Jesus during this renewal.

What is this renewal about? It is about overcoming every obstacle in your life to receiving more of Jesus' love. If only we knew the passionate love of Jesus ready to be poured out on us, we would allow no obstacle to stand in our path!

How is it, then, that we receive the blessing?

7

Receiving the Blessing

For years I found it difficult to believe, when I saw others professing to be "blessed" at meetings, that it was really happening. Why? Because it was not happening to me. I judged others by my own experience, not realizing that cynicism was shutting me off from the flow of God.

I also allowed God to bless me only in certain ways. I enjoyed inspiring messages. I loved acquiring information about the Lord and the Christian walk. But I did not go in for "thrills and chills" and was too proud to think I needed such experiences. I believed (dry as I was) that I could fulfill my ministry without them. And to worship at the shrine of peripheral experience was to demand something else from God when His written Word is enough.

The Visitation to the Doubter

You may be where I was. If so, you are not alone. One of Jesus' twelve select disciples fell into this category, too—although the poor guy has been nicknamed by the Church for the only recorded incident in his life in which he displayed doubt. It is possible to label yourself just as blithely as we label Thomas by characterizing yourself in certain ways: "I'm not one for emotional experiences." "I don't 'go down.'" "I don't think much of all this mumbo-jumbo." These easy labels trap you, limiting your realm of experience to what has already happened. Better to say, "I have some questions, but I'm open to whatever God has for me."

But it is hard when you have been excluded from how God seems to be blessing many others.

Thomas was not present the night Jesus first appeared to the disciples after His resurrection. They had been hovering together, devastated emotionally because their Master had been unjustly and mercilessly killed. One can only imagine the horror of their grief. All their hopes had been disappointed. Three years of their lives had been seemingly wasted. Already they were beginning to doubt what they had seen. One of their number, Mary Magdalene, had even been hallucinating that she had witnessed Him alive!

Suddenly the Lord Jesus Himself came and stood in the room with them, although the door had been shut tight. In wonder and amazement they watched as He showed them His hands and side. The very sight of Jesus filled them with gladness and joy, but Jesus had more for them. He pronounced blessing upon them: "Peace to you! As the Father has sent Me, I also send you" (John 20:21, NKJV). Then He breathed on them the powerful breath of spiritual life and said, "Receive the Holy Spirit" (verse 22). The next breath every man in the room drew was filled with the life-giving presence of the Holy Spirit, the very breath of God. Finally Jesus imparted to them the authority to forgive—one of the most powerful ministries anyone can have because it opens the Kingdom of heaven and every work of grace to the undeserving.

One can only imagine the awe of those moments the resurrected Lord had with His disciples. It was a powerful visitation that brought vision, release from sorrow, commission, impartation, blessing and gladness. Unfortunately Thomas missed it. (Be careful not to miss church these days for frivolous reasons!)

If the disciples were anything like us, by the following day they had probably condensed the entire experience into a formula for "receiving." When they found Thomas and told him about their night, maybe they tried to take advantage of their new impartation and blow on him the same blessing! Or, if he received nothing, they may have exercised their newfound ministry of forgiveness and asked him if there was anyone in his past he needed to forgive!

But Thomas was angry, still suffering the grief of having lost Jesus and feeling he had now been passed by. You can almost hear the thoughts running through his mind: *Why did Jesus wait until a moment I wasn't there to bless everyone else? What did I do wrong? Did I offend Him in some way? Does He consider me in the same cat-egory with Judas? Perhaps that's the only time He'll appear and I missed it. I'm left alone now, while all the others got special treatment.*

No wonder Thomas blurted out, "Unless I see in His hands the print of the nails, and put my finger into the print of the nails, and put my hand into His side, I will not believe" (John 20:25, NKJV). He was almost daring God to do something special for him. After all, didn't his years of faithfulness warrant the same attention from Jesus that everyone else had received?

Seven days passed. Jesus did not reappear. Then, on the eighth day, as the doors were shut again and they were all together, He came again for Thomas' sake. As though He had been standing there during Thomas' outburst, Jesus answered the disciple's challenge: "Reach your finger here, and look at My hands; and reach your hand here, and put it into My side. Do not be unbelieving, but believing" (verse 27, NKJV).

Thomas was allowed to experience the resurrected Jesus in a way the others had not. Jesus permitted Thomas not just to see Him but to touch Him exactly as Thomas had demanded. According to what Jesus told him, I believe he received the ability, through this experi-ence with the Lord, to have great faith.

But lest we ever get proud of some spiritual experience of our own, we must remember what Jesus told Thomas: "Because you have seen Me, you have believed. Blessed are those who have not seen and yet have believed" (verse 29, NKJV).

Have you ever noticed that the other disciples did not believe until they saw Jesus either? We receive a visitation from the Lord not because we are more spiritual than others, but because we are hun-gry and needy. It is the acknowledgment of deep need that causes us to hunger after Him until we receive.

How Can Doubters Receive?

Thomas probably assumed mistakenly that because he had not been present when the others saw Jesus, he would not see Him himself. There is a lesson here for us. When others seem to be receiving from the Lord, never think—because you have not been blessed as they have—that the Lord does not want to bless you, too. Some of our brothers and sisters give up seeking the ministry and gifts of the Spirit because they assume these were not meant for them. But this was not true for Thomas. Not only did the Lord want Thomas to see Him, but because the disciple asked for more, he was permitted more.

Many in this visitation, like Thomas, are asking, "More, Lord, for me!"

Assuming you are some special case—that you are so different or unworthy that you cannot have the same blessings as others—is a subtle form of pride that sets up a roadblock between you and the Lord. So long as you think He does not want a particular blessing for you and you do not ask, you may be deceived out of having it. Remember, difficulty receiving from the Lord is often a challenge from Him to keep seeking. This is what Jesus meant when He said, "Blessed are they which do hunger and thirst after righteousness: for they shall be filled" (Matthew 5:6, KJV).

Thomas' false assumptions erupted from a grieved, disappointed heart. Anger is a stage of grief, and Thomas was clearly there when he first heard Jesus was alive. So were the other disciples whom Mary Magdalene told she had seen the Lord. Mary, the first human being to see Jesus alive and touch Him, had encountered Him when lingering near the tomb. Her heart's desire was met beyond her wildest expectations.

But we can be brought so low by anger over griefs, hurts, offenses and disillusionment with trials that we become not only skeptical but cynical. Cynicism lay behind Thomas' angry outburst. Probably he did not expect to be visited personally by Jesus. Almost sarcastically he dared the other disciples to keep believing, and he implied that unless he, too, received an unlikely rare appearance, he would not be as gullible as they were. He did not say, "I cannot believe." He said, "I will not."

I can identify with such doubt. It is difficult to watch other Christians having wonderful experiences and not be a little jealous. Sometimes the Lord provokes people to jealousy of this kind so they will keep seeking until He answers. "Ask, and it shall be given to you; seek, and you shall find; knock, and it shall be opened to you" (Matthew 7:7). Each of these verb forms implies that we are to ask, seek and knock continuously. To continue knocking means that for a while the door stays closed. Ask yourself, *How badly do I want God? To what lengths will I go in order to find Him?*

As I have sought prayer repeatedly, the Lord has graciously rinsed cynicism out of my life. I find it much easier to believe now when others tell me of their experiences. I am also learning to pay attention to mental thoughts and pictures I used to ignore, thinking they were only me.

In all the mistakes I made in my dry season, I kept hanging around. That is what Thomas did. Even though he was angry, cynical and jealous, he kept hanging out with the guys. Maybe he did not know what else to do. But he did not give up. He was right where he should be when Jesus visited again.

Do not let discouragement drive you away from the Church. That is where Jesus promises to show up in every season of refreshing. He will never forsake her. And no matter how downcast you may be, He will not forsake you, either. Many Christians are in for a glorious visitation simply because they keep hanging around waiting for God to meet them.

When Jesus finally visited again, He told Thomas what to do in order to receive from Him. Thomas needed the faith that would come from touching Jesus. When Jesus told him to touch His wounds, I am sure Thomas obeyed. And as he did, something happened to him, for he exclaimed, "My Lord and my God!" (John 20:28). The exclamation point reveals his surprise and awe. He could not help but worship Jesus.

Once we know that what is happening to other people is real, we must do everything possible to obey the Lord ourselves. Whatever Jesus wants you to do, in order to best receive from Him, do it, even if you risk making a mistake.

How Can I Receive from the Lord?

So how do we open ourselves to the blessing of the Lord? There are at least six ways.

Humble Yourself

One of the greatest stumblingblocks to receiving from God is a proud spirit: "God resists the proud, but gives grace to the humble" (James 4:6, NKJV). We exhibit pride when we are choosy about where we will go in order to receive, or about who prays for us, or about what manifestations we are willing to receive. Pride is lurking when we are unwilling to forgive others for offenses. There are other ways, too, in which we show pride—like loving our dignity more than we love Jesus.

Surrender yourself completely to the Lord. Do not think He has nothing for you because you are too wicked—or, on the other hand, too mature in the Spirit. Regardless of how vile we have been, our only prayer is to touch the Lord and be filled with His righteousness. Regardless of how mature we are, we can always come to know Him better.

Surrender yourself to God from your heart, body, soul and spirit. Tell Him you are willing to allow Him to do with you as He sees fit. This amounts to surrendering yourself anew to the Lordship of Jesus Christ.

Give Up Your Agenda

Before the Lord saves Aunt Petunia and Uncle Fred, or answers the other requests on your prayer list, He wants to touch you. And before He heals your body, He may want to touch someplace else first. Without realizing it, you may be attempting to confine the Lord by defining for Him the process by which He should move.

When seeking the Lord, surrender your agenda to Him. This gives Him the freedom to touch you in the way He chooses. It also opens your heart to the unexpected and puts you in awe of the God who can do anything—and probably will!

Be As Dependent As a Child

Receiving is more than presenting yourself for prayer. It is more than "going down under the power." Even this will become an empty ritual unless you open your spirit to the Lord in childlike trust and dependency.

Childlikeness is not the childishness of immaturity. It embraces all the positive characteristics children possess: wonder, simplicity, playfulness, trust, naïve innocence about evil, lack of inhibition, quick recovery from anger. Childlikeness causes us to acknowledge our dependence on the power of the Holy Spirit, and not on our human strength or cleverness, to meet the challenges the enemy presents.

Surrender like a helpless child to the loving arms of your heavenly Father—even if you are 95 years old!—and let Him love you. Don't try to analyze your problems and work them out on your own. The powerful reality of Sabbath rest is promised to believers who cease striving in their own strength and allow themselves to be touched by His overwhelming love. The same childlike surrender that motivates you to risk jumping into the river in the first place will help you continue to receive blessing after blessing from Him.

John Carr, the minister I mentioned in the last chapter, is a pastor's pastor who travels around the world from his home church in Dundee, Scotland. John has been called on to confront and help resolve many problems in local churches. When I asked him how he was able to do this and remain encouraged personally, I was surprised at his reply. "I'm only Father's little child," he said. "He gives me the grace to do it." Isn't that the key to the Kingdom of heaven?

Put Yourself in the "Receive" Rather Than "Give" Mode

You may be so conditioned to give that you feel guilty receiving. But unless you continue to receive freely, you will eventually be drained dry.

You may find it easy to switch gears from "give" to "receive," or this may take earnest prayer and many trips to the altar. Rather than praying aloud, it may help you to simply focus on Jesus and open your heart to Him.

Receive the Filling of the Spirit

Set your mind on loving God. Relax. Don't try to strain for a blessing. Rather, accept it as a gift He gives you eagerly. What you are asking for is to be filled with the Holy Spirit today. You may have asked to be filled with the Holy Spirit years ago, or you may believe you received the Holy Spirit at conversion. In either case, ask Him for more of His Spirit.

God will answer this prayer because He wants you to know His love and the power of His presence more than you can imagine. He gave His only begotten Son so that you might have the fullness of His Spirit. And God knows that the regenerating work of the Spirit is your only hope for the changes you long for.

Yield

After a few moments, as you wait in His presence, you may feel nothing, or you may begin to experience some physical manifestation. You may continue to wait on Him quietly, or you may find yourself wanting to dance, leap, fall, shout or roar. Or you may sense an internal urge to praise God in a language you have never learned. Open your mouth and try, even if it seems strange. Don't be afraid. God knows your heart, and will extend His arms to you as you run toward Him.

Yielding to any God-given manifestation increases the sense of His presence. Suppressing it seems to quench the Spirit.

How Much Is Too Much?

Every few months during this renewal, I have read articles by well-meaning Christians cautioning the Body of Christ about what they consider "too many" manifestations or "too much" prayer. They seem to want everyone to stop receiving at the point they deem appropriate, as though we need to get up now and get on with Kingdom business.

But why? We have been attempting Kingdom business for years without His power. Perhaps these brothers and sisters fear that believers will begin to desire the emotion of being filled with the Holy Spirit without allowing the Spirit access to their character.

Character and the fruit of the Spirit are vital. And without love, all the gifts in the world are as "a noisy gong or a clanging cymbal" (1 Corinthians 13:1). But who is to say when we have had enough and become too saturated with the presence of God? How much of His love and power is "too much"? Is there such a thing as "too much" joy, peace, fullness, gifting, empowering for service? Why do we think we can ever imbibe all there is of our eternal heavenly Father? Why can't we allow the Lord to manage the dispensing of His Holy Spirit?

Again I emphasize that the apostle Paul and Jesus Himself taught us to "keep asking, keep seeking and keep knocking"—the literal Greek translation of Luke 11:9.

So long as the Holy Spirit is blessing you as you receive prayer, continue receiving and experiencing. As you are filled daily with the Spirit, you will notice that as you give out, you need to be refilled again and again. But as you keep your focus on receiving the love of Jesus and desiring to bless Him with your obedience and faithfulness, you need not worry about receiving too much!

8

Guarding Your Oil

*T*he renewal had been flourishing in our congregation for ten months with only mild ebbs and flows, until one week in September 1995. It seemed that week that a weight dropped onto the church.

We have never believed in placing undue emphasis on the enemy, nor do we look for him behind every mishap. But suddenly he overplayed his hand and launched a discernible attack. That Sunday more than half the congregation, for one reason or another, failed to show up for Sunday service. One family was suffering because the father had lost his job. Many others were suffering a lull, too. Several were succumbing to depression.

For months I had enjoyed unbroken communion with the Lord. An air of expectancy had pervaded my spirit. This week, however, when I started to pray, I felt I was praying through molasses. I kept sighing from a weight that seemed to have fallen on me.

Bill felt it, too. It was as though we were suddenly carrying the full burden alone again. The devil, it seemed, was snickering in the corner, sticking out his tongue at us as though daring us to rise above these messes he had secretly created.

Four months earlier, the congregation had received a prophetic word: "Keep the fire lit, for it is about to catch on in your area." After ten months of continuous blessing, we had heard of only five other local congregations (three of them, like us, small) that had been affected by the renewal. In several other churches in the area, renewal had begun but had fizzled or been stamped out by opposition. Our congregation seemed like a small pilot light on a gas range. Needed was an open valve in a few more churches and a surge of the Lord's presence for the fire to catch on in the Pittsburgh area. But it was difficult to remain enthusiastic and hold on for the next stage of God's blessing.

Throughout the year Bill and I had made eight trips to Toronto, simply for the purpose of fanning the flame of love for Jesus in our own hearts. Every time we went, the Lord met us with tender encouragement. Now it was time to guard what had been entrusted to us. But how?

Identifying the Opposition

The parable of the ten virgins waiting for the bridegroom in Matthew 25 carries a clear message to any church or individual believer who has been blessed with the fresh oil of renewal. "When the foolish took their lamps," said Jesus, "they took no oil with them, but the prudent took oil in flasks along with their lamps" (verses 3–4). This parable, which describes the door of the wedding feast being shut to the five foolish virgins who ran out of oil, seems strong coming from the lips of Jesus, but it is a prophetic warning to anyone who has received the oil of joy for his lamp: Guard that oil!

Gerald Coates, overseer of a group of British churches called Pioneer People, offers four strong conclusions about revivals and awakenings—and their problems—in his book *The Vision: An Antidote to Post-Charismatic Depression* (Kingsway, 1995):

> 1. Revival is for the church—we need to be revived in faith and in the power of the Holy Spirit. A great awakening is for the lost, when they become aware that God is in the land and salvation is possible.
> 2. Both great awakenings and revivals are untidy. The Spirit of God graciously blows and speaks alongside human frailty, sin, denomi-

national tradition and even demonic activity. After all, the church in Corinth was in a state of disorder at the same time as being most active in the gifts of the Spirit.

3. The Holy Spirit does not lift off when the theologically trained would like him to. The Spirit stirs emotions to purify faith, belief and experience, whereas Pharisees want to stop anything they consider unorthodox and emotional and from their point of view untraditional.

4. It is often the biblically committed who are devoid of an outward experience of the Holy Spirit, who will oppose revival or a great awakening as much, if not more, than the unbeliever.

pp. 112–113

The weapons formed against this renewal are the same that attack every move of the Holy Spirit. Satan is not very original. He does not have to be; we are too often ignorant of his schemes. Here are three main weapons he uses.

Public Denunciation

Anyone who has experienced a revived passion for Jesus, His work and His people will face ridicule, criticism and public opposition from brothers and sisters. Similarly, in the days following Israel's return from captivity, Sanballat, Tobiah and Geshem purported to favor what was right but opposed Nehemiah's project to rebuild the wall around Jerusalem.

I am not talking about the honest seeker who does not yet understand what God is doing, but the self-satisfied religionist who, without hungering earnestly for more and searching until he finds, sets himself in vociferous opposition. He may even make a livelihood from engendering controversy in the Body of Christ through a "ministry" of what amounts to little more than fault-finding and backbiting. This person may be one of the Herods who tells the wise men searching for Jesus to "go find Him for me" (see Matthew 2:8) and who makes a pretense of wanting to worship when he really wants to destroy.

Such opposition can be a sign that the situation being debated is a genuine work of God. In general, the more powerful the truth, the stronger the criticism. But those who enjoy controversy may find the effects of renewal ebbing from their own spirits.

Opposition can also ensnare those who feel they must protect a work of God from slander. Soon they are drawn into wrestling with flesh and blood—what Paul said we are *not* struggling against (see Ephesians 6:12). It is best to let the opponents alone, avoid dissension and seek only Jesus.

When Stephen prayed for those who were stoning him to death, his intercessory pleas for forgiveness included mercy for "a young man named Saul" (Acts 7:58) who held the cloaks of Stephen's murderers. Did Stephen's prayer for forgiveness contribute to Saul's salvation? Perhaps. And you are probably a Christian today because of the influence of Saul, who later penned a large portion of the New Testament.

But public opposition should, in my opinion, be confronted by leadership within a local congregation. In a large church it is more difficult for opposing voices to gain influence, but in a smaller one they are heard more easily. The pastors and leaders may need to speak with those who are hostile or bitter.

Charles Finney, America's foremost revival preacher in the nineteenth century, warned about being drawn into controversy with opponents:

> Revivals can be put down by the combined opposition of the Old School, and a bad spirit in the New School. If those who do nothing to promote revivals continue their opposition, and if those who are laboring to promote them allow themselves to get impatient, and get into a bad spirit, the revival will cease. When the Old School write letters in the newspapers, against revivals or revival men, and the New School write letters back again, in an angry, contentious spirit, revivals will cease. . . . Let them keep about their work, and neither talk about the opposition, nor preach upon it, nor rush into print about it. If others choose to publish "slang," let the Lord's people keep to their work. None of the slander will stop the revival while those who are engaged in it mind their business, and keep to the work. . . .
>
> *Finney on Revival*
> (Bethany, 1994), pp. 63–64

Those who sincerely need specific answers to public denunciations of the current renewal should read a pamphlet entitled *Revival: The Real Thing* by Don Williams (P.O. Box 1302, La Jolla, CA 92038). Williams is a graduate of Princeton Theological Seminary, holds the Ph.D. from Columbia University and has experienced the renewal himself.

Remember, no one can take away your ability to be touched by your heavenly Father unless you allow opponents or objectors to offend you. Pray for them.

Apathy

A far more subtle weapon of the enemy than public opposition is wielded within a group of people who agree that a particular blessing is from God but take the moving of the Holy Spirit for granted. They believe the Lord will always be there and that their participation in renewal services is not necessary. They come and go, press the grace of God to the limit and ignore the season of blessing. They may give lipservice to it, but their actions speak more loudly than their words, as if what God is doing is not real or is merely a fad that will pass.

Apathy is more of a weapon than public denunciation. It is the sin of the Laodicean church in the book of Revelation who did not know how "wretched" they were, or that Jesus was knocking gently on the door of their hearts (see Revelation 3:14–22).

The reactions of many in the Body of Christ who do not recognize what God is doing today reminds me of the movie *Awakenings* with Robin Williams and Robert De Niro. It is the true story of a young psychiatrist who discovered in the late 1960s that the medication L-dopa, used to treat Parkinson's disease, would awaken victims of "sleeping sickness" out of their catatonic states. Eagerly he battled for and received permission to give the medication to his patients. And to his joy, the victims began to awaken to live normal lives. But as time wore on, the doctor watched in horror and despair as one by one they lapsed back into their silent, frozen, trancelike states.

The medication proved too toxic at heavy doses and reversed its healing effects. The patients who were still awake were appalled at the prospect of losing the miraculous effects of the medication and reverting to their former condition.

Those who take renewal for granted or who do not treasure it enough to commit themselves wholeheartedly to the Lord's purposes will find apathy creeping into their lives and putting them back to sleep.

Revival is a precious time in the Church that happens for only rare periods. Real visitations are humanly unpredictable and may occur only once in several decades. So it is important to recognize it, embrace it and regard it as the most precious blessing the Holy Spirit will bring to the Church perhaps in your lifetime.

If ever there was a time to serve God, it is now. It is time to deny yourself and rearrange your schedule to prioritize the work of God.

Isaiah 55 speaks to any church or believer who needs revival: "Seek the LORD while He may be found; call upon Him while He is near" (Isaiah 55:6). This implies that the Lord is nearer during certain seasons than others. The apostle Peter cautioned us to "repent therefore and return, that your sins may be wiped away, in order that times of refreshing may come from the presence of the Lord" (Acts 3:19). The phrase *times of refreshing* implies the same thing in the context of the New Covenant as the admonition from Isaiah does in the Old.

Even though each of us who has accepted Jesus Christ as Savior has a deposit of the Holy Spirit within, we can also be blessed during seasons when the Lord's visitation presence draws especially near. Signs and wonders increase and the Holy Spirit moves powerfully to change lives and situations that only weeks before seemed impossible. Believers are filled with new life and joy. To ignore such a season or to partake of it with less than full devotion causes deep grief to God and discouragement to His people.

A season of visitation is a time not to "[forsake] our own assembling together" (Hebrews 10:25) or to substitute the mundane pursuits of life for the precious presence of the Lord. Those so tempted must remember the words of Jesus to Jerusalem: "How often I wanted to gather your children together, the way a hen gathers her chicks under her wings, and you were unwilling" (Matthew 23:37).

The ones who make themselves continuous "receivers," who do not make trips to the altar an empty ritual, will find themselves filled and filled again with the Holy Spirit and will avoid the apathy that settles in on those who do not. And unless we make our renewal top priority, we will have trouble with the third tool of the enemy.

Discouragement

Unless we guard the presence of the Holy Spirit within, we may relapse (like the patients in *Awakenings)* into not only apathy but discouragement. I fear this weapon of the enemy most of all.

Before the present renewal, continual disappointment had all but quenched the Holy Spirit in me. The ministry had become a religious hell. Then the Lord sent refreshing into my heart and revived what Isaiah called a "dimly burning wick" (Isaiah 42:3).

Jack Groblewski, the Bethlehem, Pennsylvania, pastor I mentioned earlier, describes in a more humorous way how he had felt: "Before the renewal, one day I had an elders' meeting and a dental appointment. I knew things were bad when I realized I was looking forward more to the dental appointment than the elders' meeting!"

He is not alone. Thousands of desperate pastors from all over the world have made their way to Toronto in the hopes that God would meet them. During trials of their faith, they had lost their passion for Jesus. And now they have found Him.

It is that reignited passion for the Lord Jesus Christ, the ability to have a sustained, intimate communion with Him, that I value most about the present renewal.

When the enemy attacked that week in our church, ten months after renewal started, I realized it had been nearly a year since I had been discouraged. One by one, reports of discouraging news reached our ears. The enemy seemed to be pulling out the stops against us.

As each report came to our attention, I felt angry and robbed and powerless to help each person in trouble. I had no answer for them other than God's river of blessing; I knew His power could heal and cleanse them. But I could not make them keep drinking.

In the face of bad news, we usually follow the same well-worn path to despair. Once we hear the bad news, we fear God will abandon us to figure it out on our own. Then Satan comes to create worst-case scenarios for our fertile minds in the form of assumptions: *It will never. . . . I can't. . . . They won't. . . .* Anger follows quickly, which we often internalize, causing depression. Finally we spread the despair to others through vocalizing our negative assumptions.

It was difficult for me to advocate renewal when it seemed to be fading in our own church. It discouraged me to realize that apathy was settling in on the congregation, and that we were headed, whether we realized it or not, back to business as usual, or to a form of renewal with no substance. For several hours one day, the weight of depression remained on me. I felt like sleeping rather than working.

But I did something I never did before. I decided not to allow myself to become discouraged.

Deep in my heart, beneath all the troublesome feelings, the fire Jesus had mercifully stirred and fed for several months was still there. Through the generosity of friends, I was able to retreat to the mountains nearby and work on this book. I refused to allow discouragement to swallow my spirit and quench the flame. And as I focused my attention on all that the Lord had done in our church, and in the Body of Christ throughout the world, the problems in our congregation faded into their proper perspective.

It was then that the Lord began to speak to me and show me my heart. He had brought me to a sense of despair about trusting in the arm of flesh. Neither Bill nor I could fan the flames of renewal in our own strength. We had come to a place of abject poverty of spirit. There were no substitutes for real visitation, nor could we support it with our own efforts. It had to be a work of the Holy Spirit: "'Not by might nor by power, but by My Spirit,' says the LORD of hosts . . ." (Zechariah 4:6). Instead of feeling despair, I felt hope, as though the

Lord was giving me faith that could be tested. My discouragement, I realized, had been allowed by the Lord, who subtracted from us every other recourse but Him.

Now I knew what King David must have felt like when he returned from battle to find the city of Ziklag pillaged and his two wives (along with the wives and children of his men) carried away into captivity (see 1 Samuel 30). His men were furious at him and bitter; then David withdrew and "strengthened himself in the LORD his God" (verse 6). Before renewal I had been unable to do this. I was more sensitive to the climate of discouragement without than the power of the Holy Spirit within. But now, in my own poverty of spirit, I had been blessed with the power of the Kingdom of heaven.

How to Guard Your Oil

What can we do when our personal supply of oil is threatened? How do we handle confrontation by the opposition of public denunciation, apathy or discouragement?

Keep Receiving

I have undergone profound emotional healing by receiving prayer during the current renewal more than two hundred times. The joy I have obtained from soaking in the river has motivated me to keep receiving prayer, which has gradually washed away fears and filled me with the Holy Spirit to a sense of fullness I have never experienced.

I am convinced that we do not see more breakthroughs in the Church because we allow the enemy to discourage us from continued soaking prayer. On at least one occasion, Jesus found it necessary to lay hands on the same blind man twice before his sight was restored properly (see Mark 8:22–26). If Jesus Himself needed to do this, why do we think we should be able to solve every problem in one "zap" of prayer?

Once again, Jesus said to keep on asking, keep on seeking, keep on knocking (see Matthew 7:7). We give up too soon.

Nurture Childlike Dependency

We discussed in the last chapter that childlikeness embraces all the positive characteristics of children and causes us to acknowledge our dependence not on human strength or cleverness but on the power of the Holy Spirit.

The same is true with dealing with opposition, apathy or discouragement. When you see yourself as a child belonging to God, who longs to hold and protect you, you submit readily to Him.

We cannot say enough about humility and childlikeness because they resist the worst sin of the human spirit, pride. Pride in the heart is subtle and can overtake you quickly, making you boast (aloud or to yourself) about what God is doing with you. Sometimes others will accuse you of pride when it is not really there; but sometimes it *is* there. Pride causes you to take credit for some aspect of spiritual renewal, as though your prayers brought it about or as though your sincerity were greater than that of others. Pride leads to an intensity born of effort and is the enemy of revival. Remaining childlike will guard against this.

To be childish, on the other hand, is to be proud and selfish. Instead, give away the blessing liberally with no thought for yourself or your church.

Pride leads to a denominational or sectarian spirit, which causes you to try to capture the revival and use it for church growth or other tainted motives. Every pastor wants to see his church grow, but the Lord will bless the church that does not use its blessing to lure others. Better to bless the sheep of others and send them home.

Renewal, I believe, is for the Church, but what God is doing will eventually reach the lost. Healthy church growth occurs not from "migrating geese" but from a steady influx of new believers coming into the Kingdom. Do not be discouraged if the renewal does not produce growth. I do not believe it was intended to. But the coming harvest will.

Resist the Devil

As you humble yourself like a child, continue stubbornly to believe in God's grace. So what if you do not have enough faith? Your heavenly Father does. Keep seeking Him. So what if you lose everything? Your heavenly Father owns everything and will keep you. Staying receptive is a form of resisting the devil.

As your spirit is refreshed, you will find those habits of thinking converted that caused you to succumb quickly to temptation. It is not a matter of fleshly effort and repeating Scriptures over and over with a sense of emptiness, but of refusing to indulge the luxury of depression.

Keep Believing in the River of God's Spirit

Many did not recognize Jesus as the Messiah when He came, but to those who did, He became the most precious commodity in life. Even in her grief and despair, Mary Magdalene made her way to the tomb and was there to see Him risen from the dead.

There may be times you do not feel like going on. But keep going back to Him, even if no one else does. God will provide you with places and ways to receive the necessary touch in your spirit. Recognize your Source of oil.

Guard the Temple of the Holy Spirit

Charles Finney identified one reason for the dissipation of revival: that the overeager abandoned reasonable attention to ordinary physical needs. You cannot *feel* (which is essential to receiving and maintaining revival) when you are tired:

> Multitudes of Christians commit a great mistake here in time of revival. They are so thoughtless, and have so little judgment, that they will break up all their habits of living, neglect to eat and sleep at the proper hours, and let the excitement run away with them, so that they overdo their bodies, and are so imprudent that they soon become exhausted, and it is impossible for them to continue in the work. Revivals

often cease from negligence and imprudence, in this respect, on the part of those engaged in carrying them on, and declensions follow.

Finney on Revival, pp. 62–63

While the apathetic may seize on the necessity of sufficient rest to support their laziness, those who need to hear it are those most on fire. Avoid drawing any conclusions about the status of your heart or about the renewal in general when you are tired. A good night's sleep may be all you and your church need to rekindle the flame.

Members of the Toronto Airport Christian Fellowship are urged to attend no more than three renewal meetings a week, but to go one night to their home group, where they receive more personal pastoral care and the benefits of accountability. We realized in our church that the small size of our congregation could not sustain protracted meetings every night, or even several times per week. So we opted for opening our regular services to the renewal, praying for everyone wanting prayer at each service, and supplementing these with monthly renewal weekends. The future might find "renewal venues" at different churches within a city as they all begin to cooperate to pour the blessing out on the entire metropolitan area.

Let me mention an aspect important for addicts (whether to drugs, alcohol or something else) relative to guarding the temple of the Holy Spirit: the danger of relapse. During times when we sense the power of the Holy Spirit, we find it difficult to imagine we will ever be tempted successfully again. The joyous emotions of revival are an enticing "high." Enjoy and maintain the fullness of the Spirit, but never lose sight of your vulnerability. Feeling delivered does not mean you can ignore temptation. Do not neglect caring for yourself, attending support group meetings, taking medications and getting proper rest. If you fall, the feelings of shame and disillusionment at what you perceive to be the fault of the revival may prevent you from receiving any further blessing from it.

Beware, too, of transferring addictions from substances like alcohol to food or even religion, substituting addictive substances and processes in your emotional cycle. Renewal comes to bless your spirit. Time will tell if you have been miraculously delivered. But be humble and wise about this snare.

Guard the precious supply of oil the Lord has placed within you as though it is your very life—because it is. This includes asking God for wisdom about who you need to share it with.

Establish Boundaries

The parable of the ten virgins in Matthew 25 includes an admonition to guard the oil from the foolish. We cannot find our way to intimacy with the Lord, and eventually to the marriage supper of the Lamb, if we allow others—even others who look like serious seekers—to drain us of our joy.

In order to stay on fire for Jesus in a dark hour, when the sleeping bride will be roused from slumber, she must keep her lamp filled with precious oil to light her way to the wedding. But others around—sometimes those closest to you, those who want ministry from you constantly—will try to entice you into pouring your oil into their lamps when what you have been given is for *you*. It is their responsibility to find their way to the "dealers" and purchase it themselves. But if you are unable to establish proper boundaries, if you do not know the limits of true and false obligation, you may pour out what is meant for you, and later find yourself dry in your own hour of need.

The only way the wise virgins could ensure they had enough oil was to say no to the foolish virgins and exhort them to go buy a supply of oil for their own lamps. Unfortunately, it was too late. For this reason, it is vital to be aware of the river and be refreshed by it when it is flowing.

I often wonder whether this river is the beginning of the harvest, or the season Jesus was speaking about just before He comes again, when the virgins rise and trim their lamps. Is it the time to buy the oil we need to fire our own lamps, our passion for Jesus? I believe the many signs of revival in the Church are alerting us to this precious season when the "oil store" is open and the wise can replenish their lamps.

After our lamps are filled, there may come a dark season in which we are tempted to fall asleep and our lamps will go out, a time when "most people's love will grow cold" (Matthew 24:12). I hope not. But we are being entrusted as stewards of oil that must be guarded, even to the point of seeming harsh and unloving. This means learning to place boundaries around your own supply and discerning the difference between those who will receive from the Holy Spirit themselves and those who only want to have what you have as cheaply as possible, with no cost to themselves.

Jesus exhorted us not to be judgmental, but He also urged us to refrain from casting our pearls, the treasures of His Kingdom, before swine—those who scorn the pearls "and turn and tear you to pieces" (Matthew 7:6). Those who despise what God is doing, or who love to see you as disheartened as they are, resemble the birds of the air in Jesus' parable of the sower (see Mark 4).

Hold your treasures in your heart until you find someone who really needs and wants Jesus. Then let the Holy Spirit give you the cue to give your treasure away.

Use Spiritual Weapons

Having the right heart is more than half the battle, but there comes a time to stand. This includes resisting the temptation to sin. Isaiah 55:7 says,

> Let the wicked forsake his way, and the unrighteous man his thoughts; and let him return to the LORD, and He will have compassion on him; and to our God, for He will abundantly pardon.

Allow the Holy Spirit to keep restoring to you the blessing of a pure heart. Be quick to confess sin and turn from it. If you are in doubt about whether to confess a sin to someone else, perhaps you should check with your pastor. Sometimes you can do great harm to another person. At other times confession brings closure and reconciliation. To keep sinning and trying to receive the benefits of revival does not work. It will not be long before the Holy Spirit convicts you. If you do not surrender, you will find yourself feeling like withdrawing from the Lord and His Church.

But this is a day when God is calling prodigals to return, a day when we need to forgive ourselves and others for wrongdoing. The ability to forgive is one of the most powerful spiritual weapons in the arsenal. Jesus thought so much of the ability to forgive that He imparted it to His disciples in the Upper Room (as we have discussed) the very evening after His resurrection.

Perhaps you need the same impartation. Ask the Lord to breathe on you the ability to let go of hurts and sins committed against you by others. This will keep the ground broken up in your heart so that you can continue receiving the blessings of renewal. To refuse to forgive others hardens your heart. And until you let go of anger, hurts and bitterness, revival will come to a grinding halt in your life. Is what others have done worth the price of missing your day of visitation and the new filling of the Holy Spirit the Lord wants to give you?

But with a cleansed, forgiving heart, you will be able to wield the weapon of intercessory prayer with sincerity. When the enemy seems to encroach on your joy, rather than fault-find, begin to pray. The pure, praying heart can destroy the works of the devil and ensure that blessing is sustained. Also, support the leadership of your church with positive prayers and Christian love that "covers a multitude of sins" (1 Peter 4:8). Imagine how you would feel in a place of awesome responsibility knowing that others were praying for *you!*

Learning to guard the treasure of this renewal is vital to sustaining it. Preparing to contain the blessing is necessary to enjoying the benefits of it as long as the Lord wants you to.

Now let's look at the most precious aspect of this current blessing.

9

Intimacy with the Lord

For part of the time Bill went to seminary in Fort Worth, I worked as the secretary-receptionist at the General Portland Cement Plant on the north side of "Cowtown." I was the only woman on site, the lone rose among thorns. After I had worked there for several months, processing mail and purchase orders and handling and relaying phone calls to various areas of the plant, they gave me a plant tour. I donned my hardhat and safety shoes and climbed into the front seat of one of the company pickups. The office manager and general foreman drove me to every site of plant operation—an experience that put faces to the voices I had talked to for months on the phone, from the quarry to the loading dock, and gave me a vision for the small part I played in the production of cement.

The center of plant operation was the kiln—a pipe more than 25 yards in length and several feet in diameter. The key to production: keeping the temperature hot enough to process the limestone from the quarry into a component that could be made into powdered cement. The kiln rotated slowly day and night, monitored constantly by three shifts of laborers who did nothing but make certain there was enough natural gas feeding the furnace to keep the fire inside hotter than three thousand degrees Fahrenheit.

From a small, heat-shielded window, I looked inside and caught a glimpse of the fire that made my own job necessary. If the temperature cooled only slightly, the quality of the cement would be diminished. So the jobs of hundreds of laborers, as well as those of the corporate heads in Dallas, depended on whether the fire in the kiln kept glowing white-hot.

This helps me understand now why I must stay on fire for Jesus. All our works, as we pass from this earthly life into His presence, will face the test of fire. Every task we perform out of duty or impure motives, rather than passion for Him, will be burned up as wood, hay or stubble. Every product of our lives—the words we have spoken, the deeds we have done—must be able to survive this fire.

Human beings, trained to judge according to the world's value system, are incapable of testing the spiritual quality of anyone's work. So in the eternal scheme of things, some deeds will be rewarded that on earth were cursed. Others will be consumed that on earth were blessed.

The key for us is not to perfect the products of our lives, but to make sure our hearts burn white-hot with love for Jesus. God has never looked for workers but worshipers. This is what Jesus told the woman at the well of Samaria: "An hour is coming, and now is, when the true worshipers shall worship the Father in spirit and truth; for such people the Father seeks to be His worshipers" (John 4:23). Those whose hearts are on fire with love for Jesus will produce eternal works in the Kingdom of God.

But this is possible only if the Lord mercifully touches and fills us with His Spirit. The Holy Spirit prepares us for our ultimate union with Christ when we will see Him face to face. He also ushers us into dimensions of God's presence now, preparing our spirits with a priceless sense of His fullness so that we (as Paul prayed),

> being rooted and grounded in love, may be able to comprehend with all the saints what is the breadth and length and height and depth, and to know the love of Christ which surpasses knowledge, that you may be filled up to all the fulness of God.
>
> Ephesians 3:17–19

The ability to stay on fire for Jesus is also a work of grace, then, initiated by Him. All we need to do is respond.

Firing Our Passion

As you examine the pages of Scripture, you notice that the lives of those God uses follow a similar pattern. The spiritual journey to find God and be used by Him includes a period of unconcern in which the person is content *without* knowing God (though he may wonder about Him or even be fascinated by Him). Then comes the sudden intrusion of God into circumstances—a burning bush, a visitation by an angel, an encounter with ultimate reality. Afterward the individual is tested in a dry wilderness experience, sometimes for years. Then, about the time he has given up all hope, he is once again confronted by God (just as suddenly as he was overtaken by the wilderness) and led into the true purpose for his life.

Abraham, Joseph, Moses, all the prophets, the disciples of Jesus, Saul of Tarsus, even the Son of God Himself, made this journey. Nor has God abandoned this pathway in our generation, when values and expectations create in us the false hope that He will choose a shorter route.

Sometimes it seems that successful brothers and sisters have taken a shortcut around this process. But as we look more closely, we see that the proof is not in the fruit of their lives, but in the depth of their knowledge and love of Christ. Every vision that will survive His fire has been birthed in the fire, tried by the flames, passed through death and into resurrection, where not even the forces of hell can destroy it.

So what is the purpose of a day of visitation? For the Lord to draw near to bless and refresh His Church; when the Bridegroom initiates, through overtures of love and blessing, a season of making Himself known to His people and firing their passion for Him.

Because we are incapable of generating passion for God on our own, apart from the fire of His Spirit, it is imperative that we not miss the day when the Holy Spirit brings us into God's presence. To reject His overtures grieves Him, quenches our passion for Jesus, diminishes the quality of our work and leaves us living life at the meager level of inadequate knowledge of His love.

Regaining Our First Love

Today the Lord is flooding all who are open with a ravishing sense of His passionate love for His bride. This, of all the gifts, is (as I have said) the most precious to me. I consider myself a love-hungry person before God. I am willing now to receive anything—laughter to the point of drunkenness, shaking, trembling, roaring, dancing, jumping, convulsing, jerking, anything that is not illegal, immoral, fattening or heretical—if I think for one brief instant that such antics will accompany a tiny taste of His love for me.

Why? Because I have lived too long without it.

I have already recounted how the fullness of spirit that the apostle Paul talked about in Ephesians 3—so glorious that he reached for the strongest adjectives to try to describe it—drained from me long ago. I comforted myself with the thought that I must be faithful to my post even if it meant I never felt anything again. My work itself, I assumed, was a manifestation of my love for Jesus.

I did not realize I belonged instead to the Ephesian church addressed in Revelation 2:4: "I have this against you, that you have left your first love." This was the church that thought the Lord prizes productivity and results above passion for Jesus. They were desperately wrong. No amount of preaching, teaching, witnessing, praying, fasting, serving, discerning, book-writing or church-planting will ever be enough to fill His heart in the absence of your love. So far as Jesus is concerned, doing everything right with an empty heart is not to have done anything at all. He warns those content in this state that their lampstand will be removed.

The lampstand in the Tabernacle of Moses, and later in the Temple of Solomon, was not a set of wax candles that burned themselves out of existence. It was a hollow, decorative lamp from which six stems were connected to a single, central, vertical pipe, much like a tree with branches. Oil that was poured into the central pipe flowed into the stems as well, filling them up. Each stem contained a wick that, when ignited, burned with a bright light that illuminated the service going on in the Holy Place of the Temple. The oil symbolizes the fullness of the Spirit, which alone is the fuel for the Light that brightens our own lives and service for Him. Without it we are working in the dark.

Which is what I had been doing for some years. There was a big gap, I realized, between where I was and where I wanted to be. But I could not figure out how to get back into the light. I could "remember . . . from where you have fallen, and repent" (Revelation 2:5), but I had no idea how to recover my first love for Jesus.

If everything we have from God—even repentance, the ability to turn—is given because of His grace, I needed desperately for God to grant me the ability to recover my passion for Him. But years wore on without it. I resembled many Christians going through religious motions and attempting to maintain some semblance of enthusiasm so as not to discourage others (even though my inner feelings would slip out to those who knew me well).

What I did not realize was that, for several years, the Holy Spirit had been doing an inner healing work that would prepare me to both receive and contain the blessing of a new move of the Holy Spirit in my own heart.

Ruth's Journey into Blessing

A young woman, a foreigner to Israel, had been devastated by the tragedies of life. Ruth had been robbed prematurely of her husband, left penniless and barren. It would be difficult to find another husband since her association with the Israelites had isolated her socially in Moab, a country cursed by the God of Israel. Ruth had only one relationship left—with her mother-in-law, Naomi, whom she loved. Together they made their way back to Bethlehem.

Five times in the first chapter of Ruth, Naomi said she was cursed, and that she had lost her husband and two sons because she had fallen out of favor with God. "I went out full," she said, "but the LORD has brought me back empty" (Ruth 1:21).

The wilderness produces those feelings of devastation. Believers who have endured a wilderness experience have likely seen all hell unleashed against them. They may have been tested to the limits of human endurance through repeated heartache and disappointment, and may even have encountered the last enemy, death. Maybe they have seen others blessed all around them, while a cloud of doom seems to hover over their own heads. Maybe they have suffered the mental anguish of misunderstanding from the Body of Christ. Perhaps they have given up and, like Naomi, feel isolated from God.

As Ruth and Naomi returned to Israel, Ruth went out to find grain for their sustenance. She "happened" into the field of Boaz, a wealthy landowner who turned out to be one of their nearest relatives, one who held the potential of removing her shame and transforming her future into great blessing. Boaz was kind and protective, making sure Ruth got extra grain as she gleaned behind his crew. You can tell, reading between the lines, that Boaz' esteem and affection for her increased with every encounter, although his pure heart would not allow him to think she might find him attractive.

The turning point of the story finds her having done all she could do, lying exhausted at the feet of Boaz, waiting for him to awaken from sleep and redeem her. Ahead lay refreshing.

This is where the Church of Jesus Christ is today. The season of dryness has brought us to a place of devastation, fruitlessness, utter dependence on the Lord Jesus Christ. Thank God for the wilderness that has led so many of His people to the painful revelation that only in lack and hunger for Him we will see His provision. During a day of visitation we see at last that it is "not by might nor by power, but by My Spirit" (Zechariah 4:6).

Jesus promised in the Sermon on the Mount that the following people will be blessed: those who are poor in spirit, reduced to mourning, hungry and thirsty for Him, meek, persecuted for righteousness.

But the blessing will not take the outward form of divine favor before they come into an intimate knowledge of the Lord that will fulfill in a greater dimension His promise of a new covenant: "They shall all know Me, from the least of them to the greatest of them" (Jeremiah 31:34).

A day is coming when the intimate knowledge of God, made possible by passion ignited by the Holy Spirit, will be experienced not by a few mystics whose books are lost on the back shelves of theological libraries, but by the least of the saints who will find themselves caught up in fellowship with the Lord. Then we will understand that all favor from God comes not because we have earned it through our faithfulness, but by grace alone. He has had designs on us since the moment He saw us!

So all those seeking Jesus Christ—ministers of large churches, pastors of tiny churches, laypersons who have survived every imaginable tragedy or who are simply aware that something is missing and long to be refreshed—are, like Ruth, seeking refuge in the God who loves them and has a covenant with them to restore them and be their Husband. If you are reading this fifty years from now, I want you to understand that you must not live without an intimate communion with the Lord that is ignited in times of visitation "while He may be found" (Isaiah 55:6).

And if someone we know longs for the fire of passion that can be transmitted only by a fresh touch from the Holy Spirit, it is wrong for us to dishonor such desperation by claiming that he or she simply wants to experience a manifestation. Desperate believers are too devastated to believe that a simple thrill or even a whiff of inspiration will restore them. They are seeking to be touched lovingly by the only One who matters.

Nor will the Lord allow them to be disappointed.

My Immersion in God's Love

Since I first witnessed a visitation of God more than 22 years ago in Dallas, I realize it is possible for unbelievers to be in a room in which they feel God's awesome presence and where they cannot help but give themselves to Him. I understand from reports of the Welsh revival of 1904 that fishermen out at sea were drawn to shore and into meetings where they met Jesus Christ. Accounts of the Azusa Street revival a year or two later report (as I have mentioned) that God "blocked off" an area surrounding the old mission building with His presence. Anyone who happened into that radius of several blocks was drawn into the meetings and into a relationship with Him, while people from all over the world longing for a touch from God were drawn to that place of outpouring in Los Angeles.

Although I have seen many evidences of His grace and blessing since that time in Dallas, I have seen no other corporate visitation like it. Everything else has contained elements of human effort. This current visitation, from my observation, is the first refreshing in twenty years that has not had *manmade* stamped all over it. It is, I believe, the refreshing of the saints Jonathan Edwards spoke of that is the first phase of revival, the phase that precedes the salvation of sinners.

But the blessings of this phase cannot be bypassed. It is the stage in which the fires of passion for Jesus will be ignited that will burn in believers' hearts and cause the works of their hands in the coming decades of harvest to survive the fire of testing.

Five months after the current visitation began, when I had been touched several times by the Holy Spirit's power, I had an experience that I have been able to talk about little, but which has had life-changing ramifications.

I had traveled to eastern Maryland to speak at a women's retreat. It was a weekend of great blessing. After the meetings were over, I was eating in the cafeteria when a lovely woman named Carolyn Jones, a member of the West Baltimore chapter of Women's Aglow, came up to the table. She was weeping and wanted to express her gratitude to me for encouraging her to be herself in the presence of the Lord. She asked me if she could hug me. I got up and wrapped my arms around her.

Instantly the power of the Holy Spirit fell on me. I began to laugh and cry at the same moment, from the depths of my being, in a noise that sounded like a wail. I began to tremble and almost collapsed. Two women at the table supported me, one under each arm, helping me down the hall to my room.

They stayed with me, as I felt as though I were being vacuumed up with powerful force into a realm with Jesus where I had never been in all my years of being a Christian. I could not see Him, but I could feel His closeness as though nothing stood between us. I felt that for my entire life I had been worshiping Him behind a wall, and that the wall had suddenly fallen down to reveal Him to me.

Waves of love washed over me. I understood in that moment that God had been drawing me from the beginning of my life. He is so awesome in His glory, and so magnetic in His presence, that worship was pulled from me by a force greater than myself. But it was the force of magnificent love. I had always read in the Bible, and believed, that God is love. But now I was experiencing it. The reason the Bible says simply, "God is love," is that no superlative in any human language can describe the all-consuming love of Jesus for your soul. Suddenly I knew why Jesus died for me. His love was so great that He was driven by love to the cross, so that I could be with Him forever.

And suddenly I understood Paul's statement "that at the name of Jesus every knee should bow . . . and that every tongue should confess that Jesus Christ is Lord" (Philippians 2:10–11). You could not possibly stand in the presence of the risen Lord, or even by an act of choice decide to kneel or fall on your face. Your human body has no choice but, in the sheer power of His presence, to collapse at His feet. John on the Isle of Patmos fell as one dead because He experienced such an encounter. "No man," God told Moses, "can see Me and live!" (Exodus 33:20). I had always imagined that this meant I would be afraid of God. But now, as I lay on the bed after that retreat, the force of His love was so powerful that I wanted to die and be with Him. I realized—as in 1 Corinthians 15:53, "This mortal must put on immortality"—that I have no way of taking in the love of Jesus, and of being able to reciprocate this love, in my physical body.

Oh, the horror of Judgment Day, when those who have spurned the love of Jesus will be confronted with the full force of their decision, with no hope of ever seeing Him again! The agony of seeing Jesus and then being deprived of Him for eternity would be the ultimate torment. And to know forever that all your sin could have been erased by His blood, burned away by one word from your mouth acknowledging His Lordship, would be hell itself.

That morning at the women's retreat I had preached a message about the prostitute who invaded the Pharisee's home and anointed Jesus' feet. Our only hope of becoming pure, I had told the women, is being in His cleansing presence. We should never turn away from Him but understand how much our worship means to Him.

But now I saw what *my* worship meant to Him! Before I had imagined that Jesus would stare straight ahead stoically while the myriad of believers worshiped Him from a distance. I knew now He was visibly affected, even melted, by the small words and phrases spoken to Him. He lived to hear me worship Him; He died for the privilege of hearing it! I could sense His glorious pleasure at the sound of my voice, at every cry from my lips—"Lord Jesus! Lord Jesus!" (for that was all I could say).

"When He appears," wrote the apostle John, "we shall be like Him, because we shall see Him just as He is" (1 John 3:2). The brief moments I spent in His manifest presence adjusted my thinking. All the pursuits of life were nothing. All the earthly possessions I had ever thought important disappeared into oblivion. I kept thinking, *It's all Jesus! There is nothing but Jesus!* Nothing in life mattered anymore except being in that place. I wanted to die, the pleasure of being near Him was so great.

The women from the retreat who had remained in the room were worshiping along with me. I wanted to urge them to continue in worship because I could sense His magnificent love for them and the great pleasure their words brought to the Lord. "If only you could understand how much He longs for and loves your worship," I wanted to tell them. But I could say nothing but "Lord Jesus!" over and over.

In His presence I saw that each of us has one problem only: that we do not know how much Jesus loves us. If we did, we would do nothing to grieve Him. As I realized how important each of us is to Him, and how dearly and passionately He loves us, there was no jealousy in it, for I could feel His love for me as well. *Gathering people into the arms of Jesus,* I thought, *is the only pursuit of eternal value. That's all that is important to Him.*

The phrase *the way into the holiest* kept echoing in my mind. I knew I was in the holiest—in a dimension of God's presence that had been concealed from me. But I had done nothing to gain entry. I had been neither fasting nor praying. And now I was aware that He not only approved of me, but desired to pour His love upon me as I was—His love that was pure, clean, holy and completely trustworthy.

When I awoke from this realm, the glory of it gradually fading, I said, "I will serve Him as long as I live. Nothing will keep me from Him. I only want to immerse myself in the luxury of pleasing Him."

In the months since, I have been deeply affected by those moments of powerfully sensing His love. In fact, I can think of little else. My faith is rock-hard in the wonderful presence of the Lord Jesus that awaits me. It is difficult to think I may live for forty more years until I can see Him again. But rather than dread that moment, I anticipate it.

None of what I experienced was in the realm of imagination. If it were, I could reimagine it. Nor do I find it easy to speak of this experience. I have spoken of it rarely because it was the most sacred moment of my life. The few times I have attempted to describe it to anyone, even Bill, I could not look at the people I was talking to.

But my life has been different. I continue to live in the awe of the love I experienced. And my desire for one more tiny glimpse of Him motivates me to give my life for Him.

Where is this renewal going, you ask me?

To the bosom of Jesus. Do not let anything stop you, because one moment in His presence is worth a lifetime of heartache and desperate searching. To know we will spend eternity in the presence of His great love is an incomparable treasure.

The initiative in this renewal is His, not ours. He is reviving our passion for Him so that we may bring pleasure to His heart and begin to feel His love—perhaps for the first time. How far away I had fallen from it, yet how little I had ever known of it! Not if I spent a lifetime sitting and worshiping Him all day long would I ever be able to do justice to His glory and return to Him the power of His great love. The love of Jesus is no longer a concept to me. He is more real than the reality I see around me.

For those who have never experienced anything like this, yet serve Him by faith, I have the highest respect. "Blessed are they who did not see," Jesus told Thomas, "and yet believed" (John 20:29). Perhaps a reward awaits others that may no longer be mine because I have caught a glimpse of Him.

Someone said to me soon after the experience, "Now you will see more." My only thought was, *What else is there to see?* I care nothing about visions of principalities or illuminations of heavenly scenes. All I want is more of Him. He is everything.

Overcoming the Fear of Intimacy

The night before this life-changing encounter, as I lay my head on the pillow, my thoughts turned to the Lord. In fact, I felt a sense of His ravishing love begin to move on my heart. I had not felt any such thing for nearly eighteen years, when I decided that feelings like that might be improper. But I had become so full of the Holy Spirit, soaking in His presence during the renewal, that I determined to abandon myself to Him and allow Him to take my worship to a new dimension. Now I had the sense that I had deprived myself for many years, through fear, of the joy of knowing Him, and that I would put Him off no longer. So I began to move past the barrier.

Let me travel farther back for a moment. During my childhood I was molested by a neighbor. Since then, and weakened through seasons of low self-worth, I had been afraid of certain dimensions of intimacy. My ability to communicate my love for Jesus in worship, for example, had been severely inhibited. I relied on singing, but even singing could not break through the wall that had stood between me and Jesus. I spent worship times at church keeping track of the time, enjoying and being inspired by the music but never transcending the emotional barrier that would allow me the privilege of expressing my love for Jesus.

A few times over the years, the Holy Spirit had moved upon me, stirring my passion for Jesus, but I was afraid of strong feelings and wondered, since few people ever spoke of them, whether they were even right. Embarrassed by such depth of feeling, I hid myself from God, afraid to let my feelings go since I did not know where they would lead.

But within moments of my revelation of God's love at the women's retreat, I found the ability to express my love to Jesus in a more intimate way. Now I understood how much He longed for my fellowship, and how my silence toward Him had robbed Him of pleasure. Now I wanted to do nothing but find words to describe how I felt about Him.

Music, I learned, is only one form of worship and only one means of facilitating intimacy with the Lord. He needs to hear words from our lips—words from our hearts and minds—that express how dear He is to us. It is this form of worship that affords Him the highest pleasure.

My insecurities and fears have diminished, but they have not all disappeared. But understanding the power of His magnificent love makes it easier for me to set aside my shortcomings and failures, realizing these are burned away in His awesome presence. Jesus' death on the cross removed the barrier of sin because He will allow nothing to stand between us and the mutual enjoyment of our love for one another. My shyness in His presence is lessening. I am beginning to trust Him with the depths of my emotion, knowing He will never reject me.

Expressing Your Love

Perhaps you, like me, have difficulty allowing yourself to worship God beyond a certain point. Perhaps you are afraid of emotion and find yourself quenching expressions of your love. Remember, His magnificent love is the antithesis of rejection. To feel rejected is to be deceived. All the depth of emotion He created in you is for loving Him deeply, and for loving others in such a way as to draw them into His arms.

Steve Long, one of the pastors at the Toronto Airport Christian Fellowship, made a comment about intimate communion with the Lord and removing hindrances to hearing from God. "I realized," he said, "that I had been listening to the wrong voice."

Many of the Lord's servants as well have been listening to the voice of their own wounded souls, or the voice of the enemy condemning them for failure, causing them to feel separated from the Lord, or that they are somehow not spiritual enough, or so full of shortcomings that He cannot love them. How tragic!

Jesus accepted the expressions of deeply felt love from that prostitute who crashed the Pharisees' banquet. Her demonstration of affection for Him embarrassed the legalists at the table who believed God's love was based on performance. But Jesus was pleased with her worship, forgave her sin and lifted her act of affection as a model of worship for all time. One moment in the Master's presence was enough to cleanse her from a lifetime of adultery. Such is the cleansing power of His presence!

When Paul said that nothing "shall be able to separate us from the love of God, which is in Christ Jesus our Lord" (Romans 8:39), he spoke not about an abstract concept of God's love, or the hope of it, but the knowledge of what it is like in His presence.

If you have difficulty overcoming the fear of intimacy, continue to receive prayer. You need to experience the sense of God's presence over and over until you stop being afraid of being rejected by Him, and until your emotions are released to serve the highest purpose for which they were created: showering affection on Jesus, and loving your heavenly Father deeply.

As you are filled with the Holy Spirit, one evidence will be a heart so full of love for the Lord that you want to sing! "[Speak] to one another in psalms and hymns and spiritual songs," admonished Paul, "singing and making melody with your heart to the Lord" (Ephesians 5:19). I have awakened some mornings realizing my heart has been singing to the Lord while I was asleep. Sometimes the song is drifting through my now-conscious mind, and I feel edified as I wake up.

As you sing in your heart to the Lord, the fullness of His Spirit becomes greater in you. Continue to allow the Holy Spirit to fill you, because He will give you words of praise and adoration that please God.

One day as I was searching for words, I heard the Lord say to me, *Speak to Me in tongues.* I realized then the value of this gift in expressing intimate worship to the Lord.

Peter Lyne, a leader with an international ministry who is associated with the Pioneer Team in Great Britain, told me that when he first received the gift of tongues in 1965, it was after a time of fervent searching. He had read every book he could find and gotten everyone he knew to lay hands on him. But when he finally received the gift of tongues, he did not allow it to develop, and before long it fell into disuse. It was as though he had been given a new suit—exciting to wear on the first day, but taken for granted as time went on.

Then the Lord impressed Peter with a challenge: *I've given you something very precious. Now what are you going to do with it?*

So in the coming weeks he set aside at least fifteen or twenty minutes every day just to pray in tongues. Within days the gift moved to a new depth. He began to experience a deeper sense of the prophetic word. Interpretation began to flow.

His advice to Christians experiencing the blessings of renewal today: Allow the Lord to take you to new depths.

Developing Intimacy

The revelation of Jesus' love is like that. As we spend time alone with Him in worship, intimacy with Him will develop. Begin to read and meditate on every passage in the Scripture that talks about His love. The mystery of the Song of Solomon is the revelation of the love of Jesus Christ for every member of His Body. First Corinthians 13 is Paul adoring God's love. Try reading that chapter aloud to God and saying, "If I speak with the tongues of men and of angels, and do not have Your love, I have become a noisy gong or a clanging cymbal"—on throughout the entire chapter.

As you examine these and every portion of Scripture, see them as personal communications of His love for you. Not merely for everyone in the world, but for *you*. Do not allow Bible study to be simply a pursuit of the intellect, but receive the words of Scripture as His tender expressions of love.

Allow yourself times when you draw aside in response to the stirring of His love in your heart. I have learned not simply to acknowledge these moments, but to stop what I am doing and turn aside to be alone with Him. In these moments, allow yourself the luxury of drinking in His presence, being filled again and again with His love. Learn to remain there as long as you sense you need to. This is how you keep your passion for Jesus burning with the white-hot fire that tests works of true spiritual value.

As you are overshadowed by Jesus' love, you will find yourself pregnant with the power of the Holy Spirit and the desire to communicate His marvelous love to others. This is how revival begins.

> It's fire we want, for fire we plead,
> Send the fire!
> The fire will meet our every need,
> Send the fire today!
> Look down and see this waiting host,
> And send the promised Holy Ghost!
> We need another Pentecost,
> Send the fire today!
>
> General William Booth
> founder of the Salvation Army

10

Nurturing the Blessing

*T*he Lord's special visitation to His Church is the most precious commodity of the Kingdom of God on earth, the pearl of great price. While there are different dimensions of the Lord's presence within the Church, those times when He invades our order and sets up His own are moments of power that those who experience remember for the rest of their lives.

We have noted the implication of Isaiah 55:6—"Seek the Lord while He may be found; call upon Him while He is near"—that, apart from God's omnipresence, there are moments in every generation when He is closer than at other moments. When He seems far away tests our faith. But "the Lord . . . will suddenly come to His temple" (Malachi 3:1). And in order to enjoy the blessings of visitation, both personally and corporately, we must recognize Him, earnestly desire Him and welcome any changes He wants to make in our plans.

Recognizing a visitation and facilitating God's agenda set the heart of the true leader apart from the hireling (see John 10:12–13). It is not our Church, after all; it is His. We are His servants, not His managers. We must be "stewards of the mysteries of God" (1 Corinthians 4:1)—including the mystery of visitation.

What God is able to do in any local church or city, during this or any season of renewal, depends on the discerning, faithful responses of leaders who have learned above all how to get out of His way and let Him move. It is for such leaders that this chapter is directed.

"Make Me Comfortable"

Rick Leis, senior pastor of the 130-family Desert Chapel in Tucson, made a habit of encouraging his congregation to relax and feel comfortable in worship. Concerned not to threaten the comfort zones of the large numbers of non-Christian visitors to the services, he often said from the pulpit, "Some will be dancing, some will be raising their hands, but you do whatever makes you feel comfortable."

His son, Steve, the worship leader and minister of music, saw no problem with this approach. But this was about to change.

Steve was flying home from a Vineyard worship conference in Anaheim, California, and talking to the Lord about worship in the church, when twenty minutes short of Tucson, the Lord began to respond: *Your comfort is not what makes Me happy. Let me show you how it feels.*

At that moment, sitting in his window seat, Steve began to laugh hysterically. Trying to conceal what was happening from the woman in the seat next to him, he hid his face in the window. That worked for ten minutes. Then the Holy Spirit overcame him so powerfully that he could not contain his laughter.

By this time he was attracting the attention of the flight attendants, one of whom offered him lozenges, apparently thinking he had been drinking. The Lord said to him, *Are you comfortable now?*

By the time the passengers were deplaning, Steve was laughing so hard he had to be helped to the door by the attendants. Then he was on his own. He made it to the end of the ramp, but collapsed to the floor at the gate, where his parents were waiting.

Rick Leis, a conservative, dignified senior pastor, told Steve later that all he wanted to do was get out of there. The waiting area was crammed with people. But the peace of God came on Rick and he laid his hand on his son and began to pray.

At that moment a couple they did not know came up to them and said, while Steve convulsed on the floor with laughter, "He must have been to the Vineyard conference." Soon people in the terminal started breaking out in laughter—most of them presumably unbelievers. (Possibly they were not as offended by the manifestation of laughter as many Christians would have been.)

What did this pastor and worship leader take away from this experience? Just before the plane landed, the Lord said to Steve, *It's not what makes you comfortable; it's what makes Me comfortable.* Then Steve realized that church leaders are to create an atmosphere in the church that is comfortable for the Lord, and that He will bring the blessing they desire.

King David's Lesson

God is speaking to leaders today in the same way He spoke to King David when he tried to bring the Ark of the Covenant back to Jerusalem on an oxcart. Without asking the counsel of the priests or following God's instructions for transporting this sacred piece of Tabernacle furniture (see Exodus 25:13–15), David committed one of the greatest sins leaders make: the sin of assuming.

Placing the golden Ark, the symbol of God's presence, on a brand-new manmade conveyance seemed a convenient, even respectful way to transport the Ark back to Jerusalem. No one would get tired carrying it, and everyone would be free to participate in the celebration.

David planned the festivities and looked forward to the day the Lord's presence would return to Jerusalem. From childhood he had been a worshiper and seeker of the Lord. No doubt he took pleasure in being the leader under whose direction the glory of God would return.

The festive parade began—instruments playing, people cheering, worshiping, dancing, singing. Then, without warning, the oxen stumbled on the rough terrain. The precious Ark began to slide. Acting instinctively to prevent its fall, a man named Uzzah lunged for the Ark to help it back onto the cart. Instantly he fell dead.

The festivities came to an abrupt halt. David's heart was filled with anger and fear. Not only had the Lord not blessed the celebration, but His "outburst" (2 Samuel 6:8) had claimed the life of one of David's subjects. The king cried out, "How can the ark of the LORD come to me?" (verse 9).

Until learning the answer, he decided to leave the troublesome piece of furniture, protected jealously by God's power, in the house of one of the priests. It would be three months before David had the courage to try again.

We will pick up the story again later in this chapter. But the lesson David learned is that God's ways were above his. No amount of good intentions could compensate for David's failure to find out how God wanted the Ark returned.

When the Church is not experiencing visitation, anything goes. We may think God does not really care how we do things, so long as our intentions are right. We may immerse ourselves in methods that *seem* permissible; after all, they result in good fruit. But when the power of God invades our lives, we are challenged with the knowledge that we cannot continue as we have. In fact, our previously trusted order against the backdrop of a new awareness of what God is capable of doing looks like a pitiful substitute.

The embarrassing nature of the manifestations that accompany the wonderful blessings of God's present visitation has produced a similar effect to the Lord's disconcerting "outburst" in David's procession: Some people are frightened, others are angry or disgusted. God is testing leaders to see if they are willing, whatever the cost, to make room for Him.

Are we ready to alter our programs to allow the Holy Spirit to move as He wills? The Lord's visitation is like precious seed that must find receptive, fertile soil in order to bear the fullest fruit. But the first consideration must be the cost.

Paying the Price: Giving Up Control

God is not an abusive Father, so temperamental and difficult to please that we must walk on eggshells to keep from offending Him.

But we must decide whether His presence is important enough to risk offending people and perhaps losing them.

People naturally resist change. Some, because of emotional abuse, pride or rigidity, fight change more than others. They search the Scriptures to attempt to support their position that the changes being made are not godly. These are the people Jesus spoke about who taste the new wine and say, "The old is good enough" (Luke 5:39).

Leaders must be confident they are acting out of obedience to the Lord, yet gentle in their approach to their parishioners. This is no time to display arrogance or imply that anyone reluctant to jump into the river is unspiritual or does not love God. Many sincere believers simply need time to process what they are seeing, examine the Scriptures, be assured that God is moving and open themselves to it. (More about this in the next section.) But there will be frustrating times when leaders must press ahead for the sake of those who long for more, while continuing to refrain from judging those who do not accept the new thing God is doing. You cannot sacrifice the hungry sheep for those who prefer to stay behind.

Leaders who fear losing tithers or church members will drag their feet until the visitation passes, hoping to avoid controversy. Note the following observation made by Jonathan Edwards in the eighteenth century about people who spend too long waiting to see the outcome and try to inspect every fruit before committing themselves to receiving the benefits of revival:

> It is probable that many of those who are thus waiting know not for what they are waiting. If they wait to see a work of God without difficulties and stumbling-blocks, it will be like a fool's waiting at the river side to have the water all run by. A work of God without stumbling-blocks is never to be expected. "It must needs be that offenses come." There never yet was any great manifestation that God made of himself to the world, without many difficulties attending it.
>
> "Distinguishing Marks of the Work of the Spirit of God," p. 133

Other leaders, particularly senior pastors, may be proud of their liturgy or order of service and enjoy retaining firm control. In resisting a new move of God, they may throw the reason off on trying not to offend people, while the real reason is they prize their pulpits. Ask yourself, *Are the services of my church merely venues for creative expression, or places where people are being filled with the Holy Spirit?*

Peter Lyne, the leader I mentioned in the last chapter who is associated with the Pioneer Team in Britain, was a physical education instructor before entering the ministry. During a renewal meeting at his church, Peter was prayed for by his wife and David Holden, who had been speaking at the meeting that night. Suddenly he found himself on the floor and—for more than an hour, to the amusement of the people in church—making swimming motions.

Peter was seeing a vision of himself swimming in Ezekiel's river. But as he swam he heard the Lord say, *Get your feet off the bottom.*

From his years as a physical education instructor, he had seen children who were making all the motions of learning to swim, but who were keeping one foot glued to the bottom of the pool.

For many years pastors and leaders who have looked as though they were swimming were still keeping one foot on the bottom.

The Lord continued, *For many years you've stepped in and stepped out and retained control. Now get your feet off the bottom. I want to be in control. I want this river to take you where I want you to go.*

Indeed, the control issue represents one of the major blockages to a move of the Holy Spirit within a church. Whether exercised by a pastor or by members of a congregation, the desire to keep tethered to a secure position may work for a while, but you cannot continue to follow what God is doing without releasing yourself to the flow and trusting Him to take you where He wants you and your church to go.

Some pastors feel a sense of responsibility to everyone in the flock, particularly those who have supported them and contributed to the church throughout the years. But our first responsibility is to honor and please God, while being patient enough with our flocks to minimize conflict. We must face also the fact that the only sheep we really have are God's, and the sheep He has allotted to our care are only the ones who trust us enough to respond to our leadership. The rest of those in the pews are merely spectators. If they neither hear nor trust us about a matter of importance, they will eventually leave the church anyway, and probably over something more trivial.

John Arnott knows the problem well. Since the renewal began, the Toronto Airport Christian Fellowship has lost members who could not accommodate the changes, both in the manifestations of renewal and in the altering of the church schedule. He observes, however, that regardless of whether the leadership opens a church to renewal, they run the risk of losing people—either those who do not want renewal and seek out a church where they are comfortable, or those who do want renewal, do not see it happening and move on to a church open to it.

When faced with this choice, then, shouldn't a pastor choose the visitation presence of the Lord? Once you have acknowledged that a work of renewal is authored by God, how can you honestly refuse Him the right of His authority over your flock? That would be an abuse of authority. The decision to open your fellowship and ministry to the power of the Holy Spirit may be costly, but the cost of not doing it is even greater: missing the day of visitation and keeping others from entering in, too. No leader who loves God wants that.

Strong leadership involves wise risk-taking. The only things in life worth having are obtained by stepping out of your security zone and taking some risk. And as your hunger for God increases, He will give you the courage to take the necessary risks to invite His presence, expose your congregation to His touch and enjoy the blessings of renewal.

Encouraging Those with Difficulty Receiving

The Lord's children who have difficulty receiving, but who want to desperately, need special attention from pastors and leaders. Rather than assume they are not looking for anything particular from God, invite them to set up a meeting with you. Pray with them and reassure them of the Lord's love for them. Help them work through their hindrances, if they are open to talking about them. If they are not, encourage them to. Some people are so shy or inhibited that it may take months of encouragement for them to open up and receive.

Edye had been abused by her father so many times that she neither laughed nor cried. Can you imagine how she must have felt when confronted with how the Lord was moving in this renewal? After a few weeks she finally called me. As I spent time talking with her, she opened up about her fears. I prayed for her. But several more months passed as she inched her way gingerly toward the river. All in the congregation who knew Edye let her alone and allowed her to come when she was ready.

She received her first touch of power after the Lord had been moving in every one of our services for eight months. How happy we were to see her lying on the floor laughing under the influence of the Holy Spirit! She gave a testimony the very next night about how the Lord had led her gradually to the place where she could receive. She was filled with boldness to be able to speak publicly about it. Her testimony put us in awe of the Lord's patient hand.

It is important for us to keep demonstrating love for people who are not yet able, for one reason or another, to accept what God is doing or to receive the way we do. Some are frightened lambs quivering from fear in a corner of the pasture. Let them understand they are receiving more than they realize by simply sitting in the congregation, and that you appreciate their faithfulness. Do your best to break down barriers so they do not feel isolated. Some will still not respond, but you will know that you have tried your best.

Changing the Wineskin

Jesus reminded the disciples that new wine requires new wineskins (see Matthew 9:17). When freshly made wine is poured into an old wineskin—brittle and hard, made for the previous batch of wine—the chemical reaction of fermentation creates gases that expand, causing the wineskin to crack and the wine to drain out. But placing new wine in flexible new wineskins, Jesus told His disciples, preserves both. It was His first hint to them that walking with Him in the power of the Holy Spirit would separate them from the old ways of Judaism. A new fellowship of called-out ones—in Greek, *ekklesia,* the Church—would contain the new wine, the power of the Spirit.

Every time the Holy Spirit moves in a new way, fresh wine is being poured into a wineskin. Will it be the old one or a new one? Jesus was exhorting us to flexibility and willingness to change to accommodate His power, rather than expecting His power to be merciful to our old, stiff wineskins. One woman pastor I talked to recently commented humorously, "My wineskin is so stretched by this renewal, it needs a girdle!"

The servant who recognizes that the Lord wants to visit His Church will face the challenge of trying to pour the fresh wine into some vessel, either old or new. Manifestations may break out in the services and not necessarily confine themselves to altar invitations or special prayer times. The Lord may interrupt the sermon or the worship leader's agenda. Alterations may have to be made in the program to ensure that the children, too, receive the blessings of renewal. Services may be added or ministries closed down in order to facilitate what God wants to do.

I recounted in chapter 2 that the first thing Bill did after our trip to Toronto was call a special meeting to tell our church what was happening and allow them to comment and ask any questions (although at that time we barely knew what was happening). The decision to tell everyone at once eliminated false reports and minimized speculation.

One of the questions we were asked was, "How will this affect the way we do things?" Bill admitted he had no idea, but that he was committed to allowing the Holy Spirit to have room—whatever that meant. If changes were to be made, Bill said, God would let us know; and he alerted the congregation to expect change.

We learned later that Stuart Bell, pastor of New Life Fellowship in Lincoln, England, introduced his church to renewal in the same way. He called that congregation of about six hundred together for a special meeting and began to pray for people. At first the Holy Spirit moved gently, but within two weeks all the manifestations of the renewal had broken out in the services.

Neither of our churches has lost a single member thus far, but other churches have, regardless of their attempts to be loving and patient with everyone.

When the "refreshing" (as the British call it) broke out in his church, Gerald Coates, one of the founders of the worldwide March for Jesus, realized he had been confronted by the Lord. In response to what his church, Pioneer People in Surrey, saw as the moving of the Holy Spirit, they canceled all their regular services and activities, including the children's programs, and began meeting for prayer three nights a week, in addition to the Sunday morning service. At the time of this writing, they are in their tenth month.

Children participate in the services now, and have not only been prayed for, but one night they prayed for the parents. "Parents were rolling about on the floor laughing," Gerald recalls. "One man, a senior businessman in our church who received an award last year from his company, went home on his hands and knees, followed by the police!"

The result? Cleansing, along with a more streamlined approach to ministry. Gerald sees it as a time of pruning.

"Many leaders are maintaining a terrible monstrosity," he says, "without asking, 'Where's the fruit?' Most of our activity is wood and leaves. The Lord is very strong about this. He says, 'If you aren't fruitful, I'll cut you down, and if you are fruitful, I'll cut you back.' It's not the fruit He cuts back; it's the wood, and the leaves from which the fruit comes. Sometimes all we want is a bigger, older, more lumbering tree. But it must be cut back."

Had the church not shut down its ministries and waited on God, it might have missed His purpose and refreshing.

What *Is* God's Purpose?

God's purpose is what it has always been: to get the Gospel to a lost world. But what if the Church is distracted in her mission? Gerald Coates is emphatic about the reason some churches see the move of the Spirit commence and subsequently dissipate.

"God always comes with a purpose," he says. "People have not asked, 'Why has He come?' But God's purpose is always found in Scripture. He wants to touch Jerusalem, Judea, Samaria and the uttermost parts of the earth. If all we want is for God to bless our own little church or ministry, and give us a super-duper version of what we had before, we're going to be disappointed. God is breaking through the boundaries, mixing us up, challenging our strengths, strengthening our weaknesses, making us more dependent on Him, because there is something new He wants to do. Like Isaiah 43:19: 'I am doing a new thing; . . . do you not perceive it?' [RSV]. The answer is, no, we don't."

Do you realize why your church exists, and what the current blessing has to do with the vision God has given you? Maybe God will throw your own vision into the trash, or prune it so it can bear fruit.

Another question you will face is whether your church should attempt protracted meetings, as the Toronto Airport Christian Fellowship has done. Is your congregation to be a refreshing center for the Body of Christ, or is it to be revitalized in order that the Lord may more effectively use it to reach the lost?

When the power of the Holy Spirit fell upon London's Holy Trinity, Brompton, the news reached the ears of an Assembly of God pastor in Sunderland, England, on the North Sea. The pressures of ministry had been particularly trying for Ken Gott. He and his wife, Lois, had lost a baby. Lois had been suffering from panic attacks. Then they received a word of prophecy that an outpouring of the Holy Spirit would come to their church, Sunderland Christian Centre, and that people from all over the world would come and receive from God in their congregation.

When Pastor Ken heard that the Holy Spirit had fallen on an Anglican church, he was by his own admission skeptical. Being from a Pentecostal denomination, he was afraid the Anglicans might not have experienced "the real thing." Still, he decided to go to London with some leaders of his church to investigate. Once there, the Lord convicted him of denominational prejudice. He went to the altar for prayer, fell on the floor and began to experience the Holy Spirit in a new dimension.

When Ken Gott returned home, the power of the Holy Spirit moved on his congregation. And within a short time people from England, Europe, Canada, the U.S. and many parts of the world were visiting Sunderland Christian Centre (including Bill and me in October 1995) looking for more of Jesus. The church has held meetings six nights a week for two years—powerful testimony to the ability of the Holy Spirit to sustain a congregation to give the blessing away, in humility and eagerness, over a long period.

The church's parking lot is surrounded by a high fence because the surrounding neighborhood, near the docks in Sunderland, is noted for crime. But since the renewal, teenagers from the streets, as well as organized crime figures, have come to Christ. The car theft rate in the area has dropped forty percent!

The Toronto church has seen its own crowd increase by 1,500 to 2,000 outside visitors a night since January 20, 1994. Conferences escalate the attendance to more than five thousand. The cost this church has paid to freely bless the worldwide Body of Christ staggers anyone who knows church administration. But the visitation has blessed this church in return.

Most churches, however, will not become refreshing centers like this one. Whatever place the Lord calls your church to, He will reveal His vision one day at a time. There is no limit to the amount of joy He will dispense to any Christian hungry for more. But our contentment must be found in intimacy with God, and He may test your motives as you allow Him to reveal why you want revival. Is it to build His Kingdom or your own? Are you possessed with a denominational spirit, or are you willing to bless and affirm other ministries and churches?

Regardless of the vision and purpose of God for your church or ministry, it is important that you open yourself to the continuous blessing of the Spirit. Honor the way God has chosen to come by opening your door to this phase of the moving of His Spirit. It will prove foundational, I believe, to the next phase of revival—but only as we remain in a constant state of spiritual hunger and eager response to what God is doing.

The Leader As Receiver and Participant

King David was not only a dynamic leader but humble before God. When the order of the Lord was finally secured and he felt ready to transport the Ark to Jerusalem, he set aside his kingly robes, put on the simple white garment of a priest and began to worship the Lord along with everyone else, "dancing before the Lord with all his might" (2 Samuel 6:14)—and before his nation as well.

The Lord loves nothing better than to see his ministers leading their flocks into the wonderful refreshing of renewal by receiving the blessing themselves—in front of their people.

Pastor Rick Leis, senior pastor of Desert Chapel in Tucson whose son was taken with laughter getting off the plane, had been teaching a four-hour class in another part of the church. Afterward he opened a door to enter the sanctuary during a service where the Holy Spirit was being poured out on the youth of the church. There in front of him was a somber young man who previously had given little outward sign of involvement. Now he was drunk in the Spirit and was standing in Pastor Rick's path. When he touched the young man on the shoulder, Pastor Rick, normally a very conservative person, found himself at the front of the auditorium, sidling down the wall of the sanctuary, collapsing to the floor, laughing hysterically. Every time he thought it was over, he tried to stand up and another wave hit him. It felt to Rick as if he had been slain in the Spirit. A wave of peace swept over him and the joy of the Lord welled up inside. This went on for a half-hour as the youthful congregation looked on, enjoying every moment of it.

"It was the Lord making a statement to the church," he says, "that what He wanted to do was O.K. They know me and they trust me."

David Holden oversees the more than one hundred churches of the New Frontiers ministry fellowship in the United Kingdom. He was touched by the Holy Spirit at a Rodney Howard-Browne meeting in St. Louis, where he fell onto the carpet and rested in the presence of the Lord. Before that moment David had only fallen once in the Spirit, at which time he told God that if He wanted to impart anything new, he wanted to receive it.

A week later, when David returned to England, he shared with his leaders and churches about the renewal he had experienced. Then all the phenomena associated with the current blessing began to break out spontaneously in every meeting where he and his team shared. David's own life, his marriage, children, ministry—all have been deeply affected by the current renewal.

"Before the present move of the Spirit," he says, "there were a lot of pressures in my life and ministry for which I was looking to my own resources to find solutions. Since being touched by the Holy Spirit, I feel those weights have been lifted from my shoulders. The difficulties and problems are still there, but my perspective of looking at them has changed. I have a new ability to give these things to God by faith. I feel I have become very serious-minded, and have had a remarkable refreshing in the joy of the Lord, which has meant that my appreciation of my salvation and all the fundamentals of the Christian life have been renewed."

In training his leaders to respond to the move of the Spirit, David Holden encourages them to be not spectators but enthusiastic participants:

> At our church in Sidcup [England] we believe that God wants to impart to us leaders so that we can bless His people. That's why we're at the forefront of this move of the Spirit. At least one of us will stay "sober"—because that gives security to the congregation. But the rest of us just plunge in. The church takes its cue from us. People are thrilled to bits when they see us receiving the Spirit and staggering round almost incapable of doing anything—and enjoying every minute.
>
> *From Refreshing to Revival*
> (Kingsway, 1995), p. 57

But receiving prayer and ministry is humbling. A leader runs the risk of being misunderstood, losing the respect of the more dignified in the congregation. King David danced so hard in front of the Lord as he was anointed by the Holy Spirit that he humiliated his wife Michal. The daughter of David's predecessor, Michal believed she knew, from being reared in Saul's family, the proper demeanor of royalty. Now in anger she attempted to shame David, mocking him sarcastically: "How the king of Israel distinguished himself today! He uncovered himself today in the eyes of his servants' maids as one of the foolish ones shamelessly uncovers himself!" (2 Samuel 6:20).

David replied,

> "It was before the LORD, who chose me above your father and above all his house, to appoint me ruler over the people of the LORD, over Israel; therefore I will celebrate before the LORD. And I will be more lightly esteemed than this and will be humble in my own eyes, but with the maids of whom you have spoken, with them I will be distinguished."
>
> verses 21–22

The text of 2 Samuel 6 follows this exchange with the information that "Michal the daughter of Saul had no child to the day of her death" (verse 23).

Is it possible that our own spiritual barrenness has been partly the result of our unwillingness to let the Holy Spirit have control of us in front of others?

When Dr. R. T. Kendall, pastor of London's Westminster Chapel and the one who "carried" the blessing to Stuart Bell, was prayed for, the Holy Spirit came, causing him to fall in front of his deacons. He wondered why God chose to move on him in front of them. Could not God have allowed him to receive in private? But he concluded, as he told Stuart's church in Lincoln, that God wanted to humble him.

What distinguishes a leader in God's sight is preferring His presence and approval above the opinions of those he or she leads. Do not allow anyone to quench the Spirit in you, or condemn you for opening your heart to the Holy Spirit or for receiving the blessings of renewal. Some will mock your hunger and say you are "too needy." Others will accuse you of being "sucked into deception." The tragedy is that people who say things like this are cursing themselves with a form of spiritual barrenness because they have yet to appreciate their own need for the Holy Spirit's presence and power.

But let's make certain we always maintain our need for Him—or else, during the next move of God, we may be blinded by pride and find ourselves in the critics' camp, never realizing we are rejecting the blessing of the Lord because, like Michal, we cannot forget the good old days. Only as we continue to receive will we be able to discern and pastor the renewal adequately.

Pastoring the Prophetic

It is scriptural to expect that, as the Holy Spirit falls on believers, they will manifest more of the gift of prophecy, just as the disciples did on the Day of Pentecost. In fact, in churches where renewal has been taking place for more than a year, the congregation moves from a season of laughing and drunkenness in the Spirit to a season of intimacy with the Lord, and on to giving it away. Many churches begin to see an increase in intercessory prayer that takes on a prophetic dimension.

Rather than praying blindly, those interceding are used by the Holy Spirit to do what I call "reconnaissance" praying. In the same way that a spy plane gathers information for battle, the Holy Spirit tests the spiritual atmosphere and begins to lay on the hearts of the intercessors specific ways to pray. As the intercessors listen to the Lord and share what they receive from Him, they are often amazed to find they have heard the same things, and that they are confirming one another's words. Such intercession done in the context of supporting the local church pastor can be a great blessing to the church. If pride is allowed to creep in, however, division can result.

When believers begin to move in a prophetic dimension, more pastoring, not less, is required. Intercessors and those with prophetic gifts need to understand that they are part of the directional ministry of the church and must operate alongside other ministries under the authority of the pastor. The days of the prophet as the only voice of God in Israel went out with John the Baptist. Now the fivefold ministry (see Ephesians 4:11–12) governs the Church; and any local church is governed by some form of authority.

At the Toronto Airport Christian Fellowship, those who want to develop their prophetic gifts are given the opportunity to attend teachings and seminars designed to help them learn to hear the voice of God. As prophetic voices with tested ministry emerge, the pastors choose to meet with them as a group every two weeks. The pastors meet with the intercessors more frequently, listening to what they have to say, and for confirmation to what they have been hearing from God themselves. The pastors carry the final responsibility to determine the direction for the church, but they make room for and nurture the ministries God has placed in their care.

While parishioners learn to develop these gifts, they often allow words to filter through their own emotional needs. Gentle correction in love will point them to using their gifts for the building up of the Church rather than for purposes of correction or condemnation.

The Power of Honest Testimony

The sense of awe that accompanies revival is the element that attracts believers to the Lord, to fellowship with other believers and to sharing Him boldly with others. This was true with the believers in the book of Acts:

> They were continually devoting themselves to the apostles' teaching and to fellowship, to the breaking of bread and to prayer. *And everyone kept feeling a sense of awe;* and many wonders and signs were taking place through the apostles.
>
> Acts 2:42–43 (italics added)

But it is possible to take the Lord's wonders for granted, His visitation presence as something that will always be there. When it becomes commonplace to see laughing in the Spirit, manifestations of the gifts and people falling under the power, the sense of awe will diminish before long. So we must guard the refreshing sense of the Lord's presence that has brought believers to long after Him so single-mindedly that they sacrifice ordinary pursuits to be in His presence.

When I asked pastors in Britain and the U.S. about sustaining a move of the Holy Spirit, almost all spoke of the power of honest testimony from members of the congregation or even from newcomers being touched. "Let the redeemed of the LORD say so, whom He has redeemed from the hand of the enemy" (Psalm 107:2, NKJV). When believers experiencing a lull in spiritual activity hear of wonderful touches from God that others are receiving, they are encouraged to learn that God has not withdrawn the corporate sense of His presence simply because *they* are having a bad day.

The story of one man in our congregation offers an example of honest testimony. One Saturday morning, after renewal had been progressing at Church of the Risen Saviour for about six months, the phone rang. I recognized the depressed voice of a wayward sheep on the other end.

Bill Westerberg had once been on our worship team, but a relapse into alcoholism had drained him of his desire to follow Jesus. He had not been to church more than five times in eight years. One of these times was two weeks before, when he had come to hear his mother testify that she had been touched by the Lord's renewing presence. Almost reluctantly Bill came up for prayer. Nothing outward happened.

Now Bill told me on the phone that, in the two weeks since receiving prayer, his mind had been filled with promises the Lord had made to him while he had been walking with Him more closely. He could not get these promises out of his thoughts.

"Do you think now could be the time God will start moving in my life?" he asked me.

I do not recommend my response to him as a model; I can only tell you what I did. I started to laugh, and kept laughing as long as

Bill kept talking. Nevertheless, by the end of the conversation (which admittedly became one-sided), Bill seemed somewhat lifted.

That evening he phoned again, this time to talk with my husband. He spilled out the following account.

After his conversation with me, he had decided that if this was to be his last time to drink, he would make a day of it. So he did, drinking all that Saturday in the upstairs apartment he rents in his sister's house.

Bill is a depressive alcoholic who when drinking turns somber, moody, pessimistic. But about seven in the evening he began to laugh. In fact, he could not stop laughing. He laughed so hard he was afraid his sister downstairs would hear him, so he stuck his head under the couch to muffle the sound.

She came upstairs anyway. "Bill, what's wrong with you?"

"There's nothing wrong with me," he said. "God is touching me."

And so He was. The love of God was consuming Bill Westerberg and drawing him back to Himself.

He sobered up instantly. Then, having regained his composure, he called my husband.

The very next morning in church he gave a powerful testimony in front of the congregation—just the facts of what had happened to him. He said he wanted to come back to church. And the church welcomed Bill with open arms.

That was more than nine months ago. Bill has come to practically every service. He did have a relapse with alcoholism, but decided this time not to let go of the Lord, since the Lord had shown Bill He had never let go of him. He has gotten involved in a recovery program to deal with his alcoholism, attends support groups as well as church, and continues to be filled at every service with the new wine of the Spirit.

Bill's testimony is, for me, one of the most powerful of the renewal because it is honest. To have testified the first day that he was totally delivered of alcohol would have brought reproach to the Gospel. Instead he recounted only the facts. Our congregation, aware of Bill's struggle, continues to pray for him to gain complete victory. But we accept him in the meantime and are allowing God time to heal Bill.

He has turned his face to the Lord and needs grace from us to make it. His testimony continues to unfold.

Urge people to testify in a way that minimizes irrelevant details but centers on the way God's power touched their lives. Also, appoint someone whose discernment you trust to talk to people who are receiving at the meetings but who are reticent about sharing publicly. Invite these people to share in three to five minutes what a touch from God has meant to them—anything from the gentle sense of His presence returning to a dry soul, to a miraculous healing, to the salvation of a loved one. You might even consider taking a midweek meeting to describe how to give a testimony that glorifies not some outward manifestation but the Lord Jesus Christ.

Lay hands on those who have testified and pray for the Holy Spirit's power to be strengthened in their lives: "More, Lord!"

Allowing people to testify can be risky. But God can be glorified best by those who love Him most, and their awe will be imparted to members of the congregation.

Too much analysis wrings the awe out of what God is doing. The truth is, we cannot tell by externals what God is doing with other people. To overanalyze leads to judgment, labeling certain things as psychological or assessing them as unnecessary. We all want what is real, but we must take care that, when discouraged, we not become cynical and lose our childlike receptivity to what God is doing. Leaders simply need to highlight what they know is real and encourage it. What is fleshly will eventually fall off. But if we are so perfectionistic that we cannot allow for mistakes, the Holy Spirit will be quenched and people who cannot testify perfectly the first time around will never learn to be free.

I do not foresee a day when we will *not* need to open up our little hearts to our heavenly Father and drink in the joy of His presence. "Let's not get too mature," says Stuart Bell. "Don't analyze too much. Let's continue to give ourselves to joy and laughter—don't think we can do without that. But ask God for a wider vision, one that will push us out into the world."

How Can I Tell When Things Need to Be Corrected?

Refraining from cynical analysis does not mean we throw out either our brains or our Bibles. Bringing the Word of God into the move of the Spirit brings balance. We must have both the Spirit and the Word, for they are in agreement. It is also important to give people a biblical handle for the manifestations that are occurring. Believe me, they are all there in the Bible—and a few extra ones that have not happened yet! Teaching from Scripture also places a move of God in perspective and answers questions about its place in God's plan.

But anything that stanches the way the Holy Spirit wants to bless His Church needs to be avoided.

Early in this renewal, John Arnott made a decision not to prune too quickly. A few years before, revival broke out among the youth in his church. Afraid that things were getting flaky and out of hand, he tried to bring correction. The revival was short-lived. Later, as he sought the Lord, God showed him that he had quenched the Holy Spirit through his overeagerness to correct. He promised the Lord that if he was granted another opportunity, he would give much more latitude to the Spirit.

Leaders must make up their minds early that their own comfort zones are less important than enabling the flock to shed its fears and receive from God. Some people are so inhibited that as soon as they let themselves go and surrender to the Lord, they have pangs of regret, afraid they have allowed themselves too much freedom. These are not the ones who need correction! If anything, they need wide space and much encouragement to be free in the Spirit. Watching the leaders respond to the Holy Spirit will encourage them.

Allow ministries to develop, but set boundaries so that those with impure motives or who cannot cooperate with leadership have limited access to the Lord's sheep. This does not quench the Spirit; it actually fans the flame.

Guests attending a service to seek a touch from God need to be in "receive" rather than "give" mode. Encourage them to relax in this place where they have no burden of responsibility. Their vulnerability affords an opportunity for the Lord to touch them.

But at times during renewal meetings at Church of the Risen Saviour, visitors we did not know have offered words of prophecy. We let them finish, but subsequently asked gently from the pulpit, "Unless you are known by the pastors on the staff of this church, would you kindly hold your prophetic words?" We were not saying your gifts and callings are not real, simply that we do not know you yet.

People told us after the meetings how much they appreciated our setting these boundaries and how secure it made them feel. Especially given the free expression of many manifestations during this renewal, it provides a sense of security to the sheep to recognize a fence out there.

How do I know in a particular situation if I am trying to get rid of the oxcart (abandon the ways of the world) or steady the Ark? How will I be able to tell if I am pruning the flesh or quenching the Spirit?

If you are not sure, it is probably better to do nothing until you are relatively certain which it is. One way to tell: Ask a person later what the Lord was doing within while he or she was experiencing a particular manifestation. If the Holy Spirit was at work, you will see positive fruit, an inner healing, a physical healing, a greater passion for Jesus. When the fruit of the Spirit is *not* present is the time to correct, especially when true experiences of the Spirit are mocked or imitated in a way that disturbs others.

At a women's retreat on the East Coast, the Holy Spirit was poured out liberally one night through the women on the ministry team. Hundreds lay on the floor. We heard loud manifestations of laughter and crying. Some women stood frozen in place. Others were shaking. Then one of the advisors approached me about a certain young woman who was rejecting prayer from anyone. As I approached her to ask what was going on, she began saying in anger, "Don't touch me, don't touch me!" Eventually she had to be taken from the meeting.

Roger Forster, head of Ichthus Fellowship and the other founder (with Gerald Coates) of March for Jesus, has opened the doors of his fellowship to the current renewal. A gracious, well-bred gentleman with a gentle demeanor, Roger was educated at Cambridge University and intended to enter the Anglican ministry. But he did not because in 1952 he received the baptism in the Holy Spirit (later speaking in tongues) without having met a single individual who claimed to be baptized in the Spirit. Well-respected outside his fellowship all through the evangelical and charismatic community in Britain, he is practiced in pastoring the renewal and allowing the Spirit to move.

"We've given a certain amount of instruction as time has gone on," he says, "as we've watched things. I didn't want to make judgments quickly, so we stood back and drew up some guidelines as to how people who have had a new touch from God can be nurtured and put to use. After a while it became more evident which manifestations needed to be corrected—which were helpful, which were not."

Roger believes in encouraging manifestations, but also in helping believers to avoid habits with no life. He believes in trying to keep everything fresh.

Sometimes people just beginning to manifest what many others have experienced already can be encouraged to continue receiving from God in the next room or at the back of the sanctuary. The laying on of hands by a ministry team may bring the manifestations into a deeper dimension as these believers receive more understanding from the Lord as to what He wants them to receive.

Fellowship and the Breaking of Bread

Spontaneous fellowship, when people want to associate with each other because they like each other and are hungry for God, is one of the products of true revival.

At first the home groups in Toronto were canceled. But as time progressed, the pastors realized that, while the Lord was drawing thousands of visitors to their doors every night, the sheep in their flock still needed ministry and accountability. So more small group leaders have been trained, and church growth (measured by the number of people attending home groups regularly) since the renewal has more than doubled.

What we call Communion was instituted by Jesus as He ate the Passover with His disciples. It was full of symbolic meaning since He was about to become the true sacrificial Passover Lamb. As intimacy with the Lord develops, Communion (far from an empty ritual) becomes more of an act of worship. Whether in the context of Sunday morning church or a shared meal in a home group (as in the early Church), room should be made for this expression of love for the Lord.

Jack Groblewski, pastor of New Covenant Christian Community in Bethlehem, Pennsylvania, focuses on developing Communion into an act of worship. He has written songs, developed messages and given room for other forms of creative expressions of worship to the Lord centered around the celebration of the Lord's Supper. Rather than allow it to become a boring habit, he regards it as precious, important to the Lord Jesus. The renewal has also breathed life into ceremonies like the dedication of children that often get inserted between the announcements and the sermon.

The Holy Spirit may prompt a spontaneous celebration of Communion. If so, have the elements ready. The congregation will be in for a visitation of power. You may see healing miracles, breakthroughs you have not witnessed in people's lives and a deepening of love for Jesus and your brothers and sisters in Christ that you did not know was possible.

Members Ministering to One Another

Gone are the days of a tiny, overworked core group or of the pastor as a one-man band. When the Holy Spirit moves in power, Christians find a renewed eagerness to serve. As the psalmist wrote, "Thy people will volunteer freely [literally, *will be freewill offerings*] in the day of Thy power" (Psalm 110:3). When members of the Body of Christ are filled with the Holy Spirit, they find the urge to function in the gifts God has given them. The Church will be frustrated unless avenues of ministry are open to them; and they, in turn, will wither on the vine and eventually fall off. (Is it really possible, in any case, to find a church with all its positions filled?)

Now is a good time, then, to train people to minister in their callings and gifts, then set them in places of responsibility (with proper supervision, of course) to learn to give away the blessings they have received.

Training a ministry team to pray for seekers at the altar is one way of allowing the power of the Holy Spirit to flow through believers. Have them exhibit their commitment and submission to the church by cooperating with the requirements for ministry. Training a ministry team also creates a safe atmosphere for seekers, who can feel confident that those praying for them are prepared to impart life to them.

Another idea: Ask believers to come to classes about signs and wonders. These may have started via the fivefold ministry (see Ephesians 4:11–12), but nothing is more awe-inspiring than the thrilling testimony of a shy person in the pew reaching out and praying for someone, then seeing God heal!

Unbelievers in the Meeting

Let the unbelievers come and forbid them not.

One night at New Life Fellowship in Lincoln, England, a downtown church, the Holy Spirit moved powerfully. A number of people received prayer. As they left the building, they began to fall. Some were so drunk with the Holy Spirit's presence that they were lying on the sidewalk, crawling on the steps. You can imagine the effect this had on passersby. Not long afterward the owner of a local pub came to church and said, "I had to see what was going on. There's more happening here than in my pub!"

Signs and wonders and manifestations confront unbelievers with the power of the real God. Evidently God thinks so, or He would not have poured out the Holy Spirit the way He did on Pentecost. We need to stop being embarrassed for God. Let Him be in control of what people see and do not see. Have someone sit with them and explain what is happening. (In our church a brochure for visitors and first-timers describes what is going on and invites them to feel free to receive prayer.) Sometimes they will not come back, but as long as what is going on in the services is genuine, isn't that between them and God?

There is no more powerful effect on an unbeliever than seeing a once-dead church revived and in love with her Lord and with one another. Sometimes theirs is the clearest discernment of all. Let them hear testimonies of how God is moving in people's lives. This plants a seed that will remain in their hearts (as it did in Bill Westerberg's) until they open them to the Lord.

One of the most fruitful tools of evangelism in England is the Alpha course, a ten-week course for inquirers into the Christian faith that started fifteen years ago at Holy Trinity, Brompton. More than 1,600 Alpha courses worldwide have sprung up in every sector of the Body of Christ. At HTB every Wednesday night, more than five hundred gather for Alpha. People from every walk of life—from the bum who used to lie on the sidewalk outside the church to the banker in the financial district—have come to Jesus Christ and become active members of the church through Alpha.

As in the house of Cornelius, when Peter preached his first sermon to the Gentiles, these people are being confronted by the living God and given a taste they will never forget—a sign that the fish out there are biting!

The House of Obed-Edom

After David's first attempt to restore the Ark of the Covenant to Jerusalem, he set it aside in the house of Obed-edom, the Gittite. After three months David apparently sent word to find out how things were going. Perhaps after the death of Uzzah, who had tried to steady the Ark, David expected a pile of body bags outside Obed-edom's house! To his delight, he was told that "the LORD has blessed the house of Obed-edom and all that belongs to him, on account of the ark of God" (2 Samuel 6:12).

The blessing on Obed-edom's household encouraged David to take the Ark home with him. He built what is known as the Tabernacle of David, a simple tent pitched around the Ark practically in his own backyard. He wanted the same blessing.

What happened to Obed-edom? In the short time the Ark resided in his house, he became attached to the presence of the Lord. David made sure the priest participated in every procession from that time on in which the Ark was transported. Obed-edom's household multiplied with the blessing of God on it. He was appointed as one of the priests to worship the Lord night and day before the Ark. As Obed-edom worshiped, he was given new realms of responsibility. His household was put in charge as gatekeepers of the storehouse, then as caretakers of the treasury and of the vessels of ministry. David saw that, since Obed-edom could be trusted with the Ark, he could be trusted with anything. He became a man whose household lived in the presence of God.

God is calling churches and pastors today to be like the house of Obed-edom, faithful to honor and care for the presence of God in our midst. A blessing of multiplication awaits these churches and pastors. I also believe, as with the house of Obed-edom, that God will use churches open to the renewal as examples of His power to bless and prosper. When those who are afraid and skeptical look on, they will see how God has blessed those churches, and be encouraged to bring the blessing into their "houses," too. He will use them to spread the fire, and in the process they will, like Obed-edom, become addicted to the presence of the Lord.

Let's be leaders whom the Lord can trust with more. Let's make a place for Him—a place where He feels comfortable.

In the final chapter of this book, let's talk about where this move of the Spirit is going.

11

Where Is the River Flowing?

The question many have been asking almost from the beginning of this renewal is, "Where is this going?"

Where did the river that Ezekiel saw end? As he assessed its stages, I am sure he wanted to know, as we do today, where the river was going. He watched as the water got deeper every thousand cubits, the farther it flowed from the house of God—first to the ankles, then to the knees, then to the loins, then enough to swim in (see Ezekiel 47:3–5). The river that started as a trickle from the house of the Lord flowed through the desert and finally reached the Dead Sea, flowing into and bringing life to the body of water so full of salt that you can sit in it and not sink:

> "Every living creature which swarms in every place where the river goes, will live. And there will be very many fish, for these waters go there, and the others become fresh; so everything will live where the river goes."
>
> Ezekiel 47:9

What Ezekiel saw was the river of God's Spirit flowing into a sea of corrupt humanity and restoring it with life-giving water from the presence of God. The apostle John, late in his life, saw the source of the same river Ezekiel saw—the river flowing from the throne of God in heaven, bordered as Ezekiel saw it: with trees whose leaves were for the healing of the nations (see Revelation 22:1–2; Ezekiel 47:12). Ezekiel also saw fishermen along the banks of what was once the Dead Sea, casting nets and gathering in fish. What began as water trickling out of the house of God turned into an end-time harvest of souls.

The river of life has the power to revive from the dead.

The River Gives Life

God could have had the river flow directly from His throne. Instead He caused it to flow through the house of the Lord.

Jesus promised that "he who believes in Me, as the Scripture said, 'From his innermost being shall flow rivers of living water'" (John 7:38)—the refreshing power of the Holy Spirit. The life-giving flow from believers filled with God's Spirit will spread the message of the Gospel of Jesus Christ to the ends of the earth. Then "the earth will be full of the knowledge of the LORD as the waters cover the sea" (Isaiah 11:9).

Jesus also promised that "this gospel of the kingdom shall be preached in the whole world for a witness to all the nations, and then the end shall come" (Matthew 24:14). So it is no wonder that, as the river flows into the Church from the throne of God, we feel an inclination, because of the direction and force of its flow, toward the lost. We want to give life.

My most satisfying natural experiences were the births of our two children, Sarah and Bill. I recall sitting in my hospital rooms the day after each one was born, overwhelmed with intense satisfaction and natural peace. Life had come out of me, and the potential for more life rested in them. Within me had been hidden the potential for many generations. My husband and I cuddled each baby and felt the awe of knowing that something of each of us had come together and now resided in them.

Every Christian has the desire to reproduce after his own kind the life of God. Even when we find ourselves barren spiritually, we nurture a desperate longing to be fruitful. God gave us this desire; He wants us to bring forth fruit. But, as in natural birth, we cannot give birth alone. It takes two.

Out of our deepening relationship with the Lord, we will indeed bear spiritual fruit.

Mary and Martha

The story of Mary and Martha aggravates many women. Usually we sympathize with Martha, who found the responsibility thrust upon her household of providing dinner for Jesus and at least seventy of His followers, whom she knew would be hungry any minute. Then there was Mary. Rather than help in the kitchen and stick to her role as a woman and hostess, she sat instead at the feet of Jesus, listening to Him teach. Interesting, when you consider that women in Judaism were allowed to neither learn nor receive teaching! Nevertheless, Mary was in the "receive" mode and did not want the mundane, pressing issue at hand to interfere with her drinking in every drop of wisdom from Jesus' lips.

Finally Martha had had enough. She tried to get Jesus to rebuke her sister for not working in the kitchen. Instead He chided Martha gently: "Mary has chosen the good part, which shall not be taken away from her" (Luke 10:42).

Some people are preoccupied with ministry. They evaluate any move of God in terms of productivity. If a ministry is not producing according to their agenda or scale of measure, it needs to be channeled into something that (in their eyes) will validate it. Perhaps they are afraid it will dissipate if it does not soon turn into revival, if souls are not being saved right now. In any case, they begin to pressure the Body of Christ to start *producing* something. Like Martha, they are expecting Mary to stop receiving from Jesus and get up and work.

Don't let anyone pressure you into such an either-or situation. Don't stop drinking every ounce of blessing you can from the fullness of the Spirit in this day of visitation. Experience everything God has for you. Develop the habit of being filled continuously with the Holy Spirit. Only out of intimacy with the Lord will you see true spiritual fruit.

As you abide in Jesus and your love for Him matures, you will find yourself hungry to do the work of the ministry He calls you to and bear fruit. But give Him the liberty of setting your work in front of you and revealing His vision for you. And whatever you do, continue allowing His life to flow through you. Straining at fruit-bearing will only produce extra fruitless growth that will have to be pruned away, while the tree planted by the river of God "yields its fruit in its season" (Psalm 1:3).

Many who started out walking in step with the Holy Spirit have thought, *Oh, no, I don't have a ministry! I'm not winning my quota of souls!* Though they began right, they tried to channel the river of the Spirit into their own visions and projects, and were disappointed when the flow dried up.

Even God's most trustworthy friends have made this mistake. Abraham, the friend of God, the patriarch of natural and spiritual Israel, found it difficult to wait for God to fulfill His promise to give him a son. He and Sarah decided to have a child through Hagar, Sarah's Egyptian maid. Then, for thirteen years, God let Abraham think Ishmael was the fulfillment of the promise, until He said to Abraham, in effect, "No, I meant what I said. A child from you and Sarah will be your heir. Your substitute is not who I had in mind." Isaac was born when Abraham was one hundred years old and Sarah was ninety. God's vision. God's time.

One of the precious aspects of this renewal is the resurrection of true spiritual visions given to many during a previous move of God. Some who received promises were forced to let their dreams die, unable to help fulfill them. Some lost all hope their dreams would ever find fulfillment. Now the Lord is revealing Himself to the visionaries, saying once again, "Now is the time!"

It is hard to stop a healthy husband and wife from conceiving children. It is harder to stop a river flowing. And boy, is it hard to stop a fisherman from fishing! Every one of these metaphors presents a picture of a force of nature stronger than ourselves taking its natural course. The natural outcome of healthy marital relations is conception. The natural course of the river Ezekiel saw is toward the

Dead Sea. And if you let down your net when Jesus tells you to, you will get more fish than you can haul in one boat! The only way we can prevent these outcomes is to get rid of our spouses, dam up the river or stop fishing.

In the same way, the natural outcome of renewal is revival.

How Does Renewal Become Revival?

The Church in Britain is experiencing renewal on a wider scale than has yet happened in the States. It has swept through every major charismatic ministry fellowship, is touching evangelicals, crossing denominational barriers and flowing into tiny villages. The British are asking, "What's next?" and looking as a model to Argentina, where revival of unprecedented magnitude has swept the country. In the past ten years the percentage of Argentineans who profess to be born again has jumped from 0.05 percent to 17 percent.

"Church leaders in Argentina," writes John Hosier in *From Refreshing to Revival,* "are looking at what the Spirit is doing around the world and saying, 'This happened in Argentina for five years, then revival broke out.'"

A Christian full of the Holy Spirit does not have to try to witness; he *is* one. The river of God's presence is flowing through his life and causing life to spring up around him.

There are two ways to harvest this new life. One way is co-laboring with the Lord in seeking out the lost and winning them diligently to Jesus Christ.

Almost all of Jesus' disciples were called while they were on their jobs—tax-collecting, fishing. Only Nathaniel was sitting under a fig tree when his brother told him about Jesus, and he was probably on a coffee break. Why? Because ministry is work. When energized by the Holy Spirit, it is fun work, but work nevertheless.

Ministry is no place for the fainthearted or lazy. Someone must prepare the messages, visit the sick, prepare the meals, meet the needs of the poor, organize the church program, administer the ministries and care for the buildings. Every spiritual vision is carried out by setting your hand to the plow and refusing to look back.

But there is another kind of harvesting: reaping in a day of visitation. In those moments you are not conscious of your own effort. Slight movements win souls. People are drawn to church not by publicity but by word of mouth and the power of God. Messages preached have the effect you dream of: causing hungry people to flock to the altar, weeping under conviction of sin and turning to Jesus Christ. People testify of miraculous divine intervention. Christians repent of sin and reconcile themselves to one another and to God. And the church is packed with hungry people waiting for more.

Don't you long for this kind of harvest?

The Next Stage: Unity

Several years ago I saw a picture in my mind of streams flowing throughout the world. They meandered through different kinds of terrain and cut varied courses through the landscape. But as I watched, the streams began to feed one by one into larger rivers. Then those rivers began to join, until they all flowed together. What I saw, I believe, was the eventual unification of the Body of Christ. As we all flow toward the same purpose, we will find ourselves becoming united to cover the earth with the Gospel.

But sometimes a day of visitation causes separation as well as unity. As a river rushes on, it may cut a new path or form new tributaries seeking a different route to the sea. The "new thing" God does in each visitation sometimes causes division. Leaders differ over methods. Paul and Barnabas served the same Lord but, at least for a season, heard the call of God differently. Initially this led to conflict; later they enjoyed lasting friendship. Sometimes, for His purposes, the Lord allows separation, while still using both vessels.

Such has proved to be the case in this renewal, too.

On December 5, 1995, John Wimber, founder and leader of the Association of Vineyard Churches, flew to Toronto to meet with the pastoral staff of the Toronto Airport Vineyard. At that meeting Wimber expressed his desire that the Toronto church be "disengaged" from the Association of Vineyard Churches. The chief reasons given included Wimber's perspective that fundamental differences in administration of renewal had caused Toronto to depart from the defined theology and purposes of the Vineyard movement. John Wimber did not feel called to oversee something outside the ministry model God had given him.

John Arnott responded in an open letter:

> We do want to publicly thank John Wimber and the AVC Board. This current move of God's Spirit would not have achieved its world-wide reach and impact without them. They have modelled Christ to us; they have been ministers of healing to us—we cannot thank them enough. We are not saying goodbye. We simply recognize that the Sovereign Lord is moving this stream of the Holy Spirit along a new tributary. The major difference this decision makes is that if anyone wants to know "What's going on in Toronto?", they now need to ask the leadership in Toronto. Other than that it is onward and upward for us. We hope that all discussions in media and cyberspace will reflect the continuing good will between AVC and the Toronto Airport Vineyard. We hope that all will continue to practice the love and mercy of Jesus that we have preached for so many ears. "Beloved, let us love one another" (1 John 4:7).

A harvest like the one we are looking for will not be reaped, as in the past, by a few isolated churches throughout the nation. The coming revival will require a new dimension of unity in the Body of Christ. In that day we will find the Holy Spirit setting up circumstances that will unify us in the Body of Christ with other churches with a common purpose. God will link all kinds of arms together—rich and poor, black and white, male and female, from small churches and big—and we will not break rank. God will form an army that will challenge the enemy.

Do not resist the Holy Spirit's move toward unity, or attempt to capture the revival for your own personal gain or for the fame of your own congregation or ministry. God will search those motives out, weigh them in the balance and find them wanting. To resist the Holy

Spirit will cause you to step out of the river and into a marsh of your own purpose. Ezekiel saw the marshes left for salt.

Rather, as your love for the Lord deepens during renewal, you will begin devoting yourself to unity in the Body of Christ. We cannot bring it, but we can allow it to happen by cooperating with God.

I cannot bear to think what would have happened if my friend Joanne Stockhowe, the Episcopal priest's wife, had not ignored the denominational barrier between us and mailed me that letter about the renewal in Toronto. "The water rose above the walls," she said about the days in the charismatic renewal when we worked together across denominational lines, "and we were all swimming together in the river." May God cause this river not only to rise above those walls, but to break them down.

Perhaps the reason much of the Church in Britain has recognized their day of visitation and the U.S. has yet to do so is the unity in the Spirit they enjoy. Their arteries are less clogged with suspicion, competitiveness and partisanship. The flow of God's blessing through the entire Body is hindered in very few places. Leaders there have been ignoring labels of *evangelical* and *charismatic* for more than 25 years, coming together for prayer and fellowship, even sharing one another's pulpits (often in the same town).

Gerald Coates, the founder of Pioneer, an international charismatic ministry fellowship based in Great Britain, was present the night the power of the Holy Spirit fell on a convention of 309 senior officers of the Salvation Army. After Gerald's message, he and Michael Green anointed with oil all the senior officers who came forward. Two men fell on their knees weeping. Another man began to weep as he stood. Another began to shake. A couple began to laugh. The meeting should have finished at 9:30 P.M., but many remained at one in the morning. It was, according to Gerald, "a sea of bodies, chairs, people confessing their sins."

A year later a similar scene occurred as Gerald spoke at another gathering of more than five hundred Salvation Army officers gathered for their first evangelism conference in decades. Similar manifestations broke out. Some did not sleep all night. Although it has caused consternation among some officers, the renewal has reawakened the organization to the power of the Holy Spirit. One officer told Gerald in May 1995, "We've never had such a major shakeup as we've had in the last eighteen months."

Gerald Coates has also seen renewal in several of Britain's prisons. One of his friends, a prison chaplain, told him recently that he just led his 349th prisoner to the Lord. "It amuses me," says Gerald, "that while we're debating whether or not Toronto is into some form of manipulation, or whether or not Rodney-Howard Browne is of God, the Lord says, 'I can't wait for all this lot! I'll start in the prisons, where they haven't got so many questions!'"

Becoming One

When our heavenly Father looks at every region of the world, I believe He sees not individual churches or even denominations, but one Church. The day the Lord revealed Himself to me, I realized in His presence that the issue is not churches or ministries, but Jesus— nothing but Him. A dimension of power is reserved for the moment when the Body of Christ begins to meet together. Our desire must be to find ways to break down walls and learn to trust each other.

But how?

We must become serious about the offenses we have caused each other. We must take time from our busy schedules to develop relationships. It is no use having meetings and making a pretense of unity when we cannot take off masks and reveal our inner fears and insecurities and find brothers and sisters who will pray for us and cover us with love. And we must reach outside the circle where we normally fellowship.

This renewal is helping us learn to swim in the river with new friends who are desperate for God.

After the renewal had been going on in our church for several months, Covenant Church of Pittsburgh heard that God was moving with us. They, too, had been touched by the Holy Spirit's power.

Their pastor, Joseph Garlington, has been a vessel for unity through-out the Body of Christ in the United States and overseas. His church did not just talk about love; they took up an offering for us. One day we went to the mailbox and opened a letter from them containing enough money to replace the worn-out carpeting in our sanctuary. It would have taken us months to raise that kind of money.

As the Holy Spirit is being poured out in church after church in Pittsburgh, pastors are beginning to develop a network for prayer. We are beginning to see the breaking down of walls. In the city of three rivers, a Fourth One is starting to flow!

This is the final stage of Ezekiel's river—water enough to swim in. As we swim together, let's pray that the Holy Spirit will come on all our churches and bring renewal everywhere.

How Do We Pray?

As we long for more of God, the Church will pray for the harvest. Individuals who have been renewed and are willing to swim with other believers in the river will take joy in praying and giving birth to true revival.

The early Church feared that the persecution they were facing would stop the river from flowing. But as they prayed, the place where they were meeting was shaken, and God filled them with bold-ness to proclaim the Gospel. Similarly, every hindrance to revival can be prayed down when we are in communion with the Lord.

Gerald Coates puts it this way: "For revival to happen, Jesus Christ must be made intelligible and attractive to those outside the Church. The rain of God has come; let's pray for more rain. The wind of God has come; let's pray for a hurricane. The fire of God has come; let's pray for more fire (not just the bit we can cope with). Let's pray, 'Lord, this is great, but we want You to go deeper in our lives.' If I would say anything to America, it's that the key to the future is not Israel, not the world, but the Church."

We, the house of God, are the source from which the river will flow to the ends of the earth. What God has already sent is the clue as to what He wants us to pray for. There is no limit to the amount of blessing we can receive in our spirits. He has already given us the watchword and prayer of this renewal: "More of You, Lord Jesus, for everyone."

Now let's get ready to contain the blessing of harvest—together!

Appendix

*T*he following word of prophecy was given by the late John Garlington at the spring pastors' convention at Evangelistic Center Church, Kansas City, on May 12, 1982:

Is this not an hour when the challenge of the Lord is made to the Church of Jesus Christ? Who is on the Lord's side? Who is on the Lord's side? Who is on the Lord's side? Will you gird upon your side the weapon of your warfare? Will you separate yourselves from your own agenda and from the things of the world and come to My side? I raise in this hour a new and fresh army. I raise an army that will march together in rank, and none shall break their rank, nor shall any thrust each other. I am going to make an irresistible army in this hour.

I call the Church of Jesus Christ to a new time of dedication, to a new time of holiness. Oh, you shall not make the mistake of time past. I was not concerned about your ball-playing. I was not concerned about your fishing. My only concern was, Where is My place in your life? I call you to reexamine your priorities, for I am gathering an army.

Yea, begin to look through your camps. I call you to a time of deliverance, and after deliverance, a time of Passover. Examine your lives and purge out the leaven of hypocrisy. Purge out the leaven of sin. Examine your lives by the light of the Holy Spirit. Examine your lives by the light of the Word of God. You shall not examine your lives by the standards of men. Cast down the standards of men and begin to exalt My Word. When I speak in My Word, allow that to be the final authority.

I am going to raise an army that shall capture whole cities. You have limited Me. You have seen four hundred and five hundred and you have clapped your hands and shouted, "Revival, revival!" And you've seen only three drops of rain. Oh, but I am going to send floods! I am going to send floods!

Yea, prophets of the past generation prophesied about this time. Many of them who prophesied did not live to see it. But rejoice, for your eyes shall see come to pass that word that was spoken.

Examine your lives, for I am going to march through your camps. Move any hidden wedge in your tents. Throw aside any of the goodly garments. Search your own hearts. You've cried out to Me, "O God, that I might be used of Thee!" Who shall ascend into My hill? He who has clean hands. I call you to cleanse your hearts. I lay a word upon you this night who have been double-minded. You have come and then you've gone; you have come and then you've gone. Why do you stand in the valley of decision? Make this the night that you will make a choice. Say in your hearts, *I am going to serve You, O God. I am going to make You Lord of my life.*

And then I'm going to gather an army. And yea, doth any army go forth to battle and doth not come back with the spoil? And yea, you shall come back with the spoil. Even as in days of old, when I sent the army out, they brought back with them the choicest of the enemy's sons and the choicest of the enemy's daughters. And I am going to let the Church arise as an army in this day. And you are going to bring back the choicest of their sons and daughters.

I am going to cause you to bring back the educated and the intellectuals. You are going to bring the rich and the poor. You are going to bring the black and the white. And yea, they shall come and you shall look. And I am going to say to you, "I still have room!" And I am going to scatter you again, and you are going to bring them and bring them until My house is full.

You shall not look upon the nations. I am shaking the nations. And yea, you have not seen the nations shake. I am going to shake Canada. I am going to shake America. I am going to shake this whole Southern and Northern hemisphere. But no, it is not the shaking of the Communists; it is not the shaking of the devil. Yea, My people, why will you give credit to the enemy for that which I am doing? Lift your eyes with discernment. Let your eyes look upon My Word.

Will you not know this night that Satan is not on his own? I created him; he is My devil. And when I finish with him, I will deal with him. And I have chosen to bruise him under your feet. You have read the Scripture about treading upon serpents and scorpions, and you have busied yourself casting out little demons, but yea, you are going to see principalities that have enthroned cities. Yea, know this, that in cities that have been gripped with narcotics, cities that have been gripped with crime, I am going to save some, I am going to destroy others and I am going to set whole cities free.

At this time John Garlington began to cry out in tongues. Then he began to laugh as he spoke in tongues. Then he laughed and laughed.

For I shall fill your mouths with laughter, and you shall laugh in the face of the enemy. You shall laugh in the face of economic decline. You shall laugh in the face of bad news. And they shall wonder, "What is it?" But I, the Lord thy God, shall arise in My people, and not only shall I turn your captivity, but I shall fill your mouths with laughter. Yea, your young men shall drink new wine as from bowls, and their mouths shall be filled with laughter. Your daughters shall eat the corn and be filled with great joy. Hallelujah!

I am going to move upon the youth of this nation even one more time, even one more time, and they shall come as they did in days past. Hallelujah!

You have been shaken in your health, for I shook your health, because you trusted in your health. I have shaken the finance, for you trusted in your finance. And yea, you are going to understand that after all the shaking has come, there is an unshakable Kingdom that cannot be moved. You are going to know how to stand in that Kingdom; you are going to know how to rejoice in that Kingdom. For I have shaken the nations, I have shaken the churches, I have shaken your lives. I have shaken you, that only that which cannot be shaken shall remain. The world is going to see a Church pristine in her beauty, marvelous in her power, a Church mighty in her meekness, a Church filled with redemptive power, a Church filled with the anointing of the Lord.

And it shall not simply be in one place. Yea, it has been that you hear that I've brought it in one place, and you run there, and you hear that I've brought it in another place, and you run there. But My glory shall fill the earth!

Yea! Set your hearts to seek Me. I call you to prepare yourselves that you might be part of that which I am going to do. Yea, there has been a hunger in many of your hearts. And in many of your circumstances, and in many of your churches, there has been the quickening of a new breeze that is in the tops of the trees. Yea, gird thyself, put on thy shoes, prepare thy heart, for the Lord God is going to begin marching in the heavens and He's going to call you to reckon, and call you to march with Him in that army that is upon the earth.

And yea, you shall gather the spoil, you shall gather the spoil; and it shall not be as it was in past revivals. You shall no longer fly upon the spoil. For you shall not only be devoted to the Lord, but the things you gather shall be devoted to Him.

He is going to do a mighty thing in the earth. The glory of the latter house shall be greater than the glory of the former. Thou shalt not say in thine heart, *I have heard that word, I have heard that word, I have heard that word.* For God is going to do it.

Yea, He is going to vindicate the prophecies given in this place, the prophecies given here and there. It shall no longer be a thing that you say, "Oh, we have heard it." But you shall say in your hearts, *Now we see it!* For the Lord Himself shall do it.

Bibliography

Arnott, John. *The Father's Blessing*. Lake Mary, Fla.: Creation House, 1995.

Boulton, Wallace, ed. *The Impact of Toronto*. Crowborough, Great Britain: Monarch, 1995.

Chevreau, Guy. *Catch the Fire*. Toronto: HarperPerennial, 1994.

Coates, Gerald. *The Vision: An Antidote to Post-Charismatic Depression*. Eastbourne, Great Britain: Kingsway Publications, Ltd., 1995.

DeArteaga, William. *Quenching the Spirit*. Lake Mary, Fla.: Creation House, 1992.

Deere, Jack. *Surprised by the Power of the Spirit*. Grand Rapids: Zondervan Publishing House, 1993.

Dixon, Patrick. *Signs of Revival*. Eastbourne, Great Britain: Kingsway Publications, Ltd., 1994.

Doucet, Daina. "What Is God Doing in Toronto?" *Charisma & Christian Life*, February 1995: pp. 20–26.

Down, Martin. *Speak to These Bones*. Crowborough, Great Britain: Monarch, 1994.

Edwards, Jonathan. *Edwards on Revival*. Carlisle, Pa.: Banner of Truth Trust, 1994.

Finney, Charles Grandison. *Finney on Revival*. Edited by E. E. Shelhamer. Minneapolis: Bethany House, 1994.

Fitz-Gibbon, Andy and Jane. *The Kiss of Intimacy*. Crowborough, Great Britain: Monarch, 1995.

Gott, Ken and Lois. *The Sunderland Refreshing*. London: Hodder & Stoughton, 1995.

Lovelace, Richard F. "The Surprising Works of God." *Christianity Today*, September 11, 1995: pp. 28–32.

Pratney, Winkie. *Revival*. Springdale, Pa.: Whitaker House, 1983.

Price, Clive. "Holy Laughter Hits British Churches." *Charisma & Christian Life*, October 1994: p. 82.

Riss, Richard M. *A History of the Revival*. Toronto: Toronto Airport Vineyard, 1995.

——. *Latter Rain.* Etobicoke, Ontario: Kingdom Flagships Foundation, 1987.

Salter, Owen. "A New Toronto Blessing Is Spreading in Australia." *Charisma & Christian Life,* September 1995: pp. 21–22.

Sherrill, John. *They Speak with Other Tongues.* Old Tappan, N.J.: Chosen Books, 1964, 1985.

"Toronto Blessing: Is it a Revival?" *Christianity Today,* May 15, 1995: p. 51.

Tuttle, Robert G. *John Wesley: His Life and Theology.* Grand Rapids: Zondervan/Asbury Press, 1978.

Virgo, Terry, David Holden and John Hosier. *From Refreshing to Revival.* Eastbourne, Great Britain: 1995.

Wallis, Arthur. *In the Day of Thy Power.* Columbia, Mo., and Fort Washington, Pa.: Cityhill Publishing Co. and Christian Literature Crusade, commemorative edition, 1989.

Warner, Rob. *Prepare for Revival.* London: Hodder & Stoughton, 1995.

Wesley, John. *The Works of John Wesley.* 3rd ed. Vol. 1. Grand Rapids: Baker Book House, 1991.

White, John. *When the Spirit Comes with Power.* London: Hodder & Stoughton, 1988.

Williams, Don. "Revival: The Real Thing." La Jolla, Calif.: Don Williams, 1995.

Witt, Stephan. "The Spirit Shakes a Seeker-Sensitive Church!" *Ministries Today,* November-December 1994: pp. 22–23.

You may contact Melinda Fish by writing:

Church of the Risen Saviour
330 Edgewood Ave.
Trafford, PA 15085